# WHY *GOOD* PEOPLE DO *BAD* THINGS
## Questions for Reflection and Discussion

## Chapter One: Who We Good People Are

1. "Whether there really is such a thing as a 'bad' person is a philosophical question" (p. 6). Do you think some people really are bad? Explain.

2. "Many transnational corporations . . . prefer to pay as little as possible for both the raw materials and for the labor. In the interests of profit maximization they typically seek to move whatever operations they can to wherever the cost of production is lower" (pp. 8-9). Do you know any transnational corporations that operate this way? Do you know any that don't?

3. "The colonels were friendly, disciplined, confident, and skilled at their professional work. They were exactly the kind of 'good' people we would want as next-door neighbors" (p. 11). What motivates people to seek a career in the military? How do they deal with the fact that military activity sometimes involves killing other people?

4. "Next to the [aircraft carrier] Intrepid an abandoned dock had been taken over by some of New York City's homeless. . . . We felt a sad shock of recognition at this symbol of distorted national priorities" (p. 12). Would a significant reduction in military expenditures release money to address social needs? How likely is this to happen? Why do you think this way?

## Chapter Two: Those We Hurt

1. "Juarez is one of the cities in the *maquiladora* belt of over 2000 factories that have sprung up since the 1970s just south of the border" (p. 23). Have you ever been to a Third World country or know anybody who has? How do you react to the living conditions of most of the people in these places?

2. ". . . clothing factories in Bangkok routinely employed children to operate the manufacturing machinery. . . . When a child slipped and got a hand or foot caught in the works, the injured boy or girl was simply carried out of the factory and laid on the sidewalk" (p. 25). Does this scene have any effect on your decision to buy clothes with the label "Made in Thailand"?

3. "Weapons manufactured in Israel, the United States, Russia, Belgium, and elsewhere are provided generously when policy or prices dictate" (p. 28). What is your attitude toward arms sales as a foreign policy tool? What about arms sales as a boost to the producing country's economy?

4. ". . . Fidel Castro, in his provocative way of going to the heart of the matter, had issued a call to Third World countries to close their books on all debt owed the First World. Wipe the slate clean, he said" (p. 29). How should the international debt owed by many Third World countries be handled?

## Chapter Three: Why We Do These Things

1. "Our culture embodies a strong belief that if it can be built, it should be built. And if it can't be built yet, let's get to work and figure out what it takes to build it tomorrow" (p. 36). Should any limits at all be set on technological advance? By whom? On what grounds?

2. ". . . another force driving good people to do bad things is the attraction of power. The ability to control our surroundings, to make others conform to our wishes, is deep and can be deadly" (p. 41). Why is power dangerous? Can the desire for power be put to good use?

3. "Some ideologies are actually committed to life-destruction, as was the Nazi super-race belief that inferior peoples must be exterminated" (p. 46). How can one tell that one's own personal philosophy of life, one's ideology, is healthy or harmful? What are the norms for judging?

4. "Dorothy Day, when it was suggested that she, too, could receive the honor of sainthood, replied, 'They can't dismiss me that easily'" (p. 48). Of what value are saints after they are dead? What is the implication of Dorothy Day's remark?

## Chapter Four: The Shadow Knows

1. "Because our unacknowledged Shadow is there as a bottled-up energy, it can suddenly impel us to hurtful and destructive actions that in a more controlled moment we wouldn't want to do" (p. 52). Find stories in a recent newspaper to which this quote might apply.

2. "More than likely, we'll find in our enemies the very characteristics in our own makeup that we have covered over or masked from view" (p. 54). Think of several enemies, personal or national. What makes them enemies? Why are they disliked?

3. "We're becoming uncomfortably accustomed to similar sights [rampaging through the streets, shouting obscenities, breaking windows, beating up bystanders] in this country, following not a loss but a victory—when a team wins the World Series, the Super Bowl, or the NBA playoffs" (p. 57). What is your reaction to this? Why do you think this is happening?

4. "What we're after is getting to know our Shadow, not necessarily eliminating its contents" (p. 59). How can one know one's Shadow better? Why not be concerned about eliminating its contents?

## Chapter Five: The S-Word

1. "Many concerned observers feel that the sexual revolution, although valuable in breaking down taboos and opening up new richness in human relationships, has gone too far" (p. 62). Where do you see evidences of the sexual revolution? Do you agree that it has been of some value? In which areas has it gone too far?

2. "Paul Brown, a Presbyterian minister and seminary professor, observed, 'The S-word is rarely mentioned in worship'" (p. 63). How do you feel about including references to human sexuality in public prayer and worship?

3. "The emotional and spiritual wounds suffered when homosexual men and women are marginalized or rejected can be more damaging than bodily wounds inflicted by physical violence" (p. 65). Do you know anyone who is

homosexual? Would you be in favor of removing all laws and public regulations that discriminate against homosexual people? Why?

4. "Gay bashing, sexual racism, and exploitation around military bases are shrugged off as necessary, although unpleasant, facts of life" (p. 71). What would it take to have a national military force that does not foster sexual exploitation?

## Chapter Six: Personal Salvation

1. "Salvation begins while a person is still struggling with this present life. It increases as one continues along the way prescribed by the religion in the confidence that this way is the right one for *me*" (p. 76). Does your understanding of salvation include action to help improve society? Do you know people for whom it does not? Why does it for some, and not for others?

2. "'Rugged individualism,' extolled in the American myth, permeates much of our culture, including our religion" (pp. 79-80). What advantages have come from the American stress on individualism? What drawbacks?

3. "Our personal video screen separates us from others watching their own personal video screens. Our personal computer absorbs us with its fascinating challenge to our creative ingenuity but in isolation from other human beings" (p. 82). If success in today's world demands computer literacy, what concomitant dangers need to be kept in mind?

4. "Personal-salvation religion can be a soothing antidote to the pain of poverty. It can also siphon off energy to improve the social environment" (p. 83). What advice would you give missionaries in Third World countries?

## Chapter Seven: Bad Faith and Good Faith

1. "A measure of desensitization is imperative to maintain our mental balance. We have to avoid being overwhelmed by too much bleakness in these nervous times" (p. 90). What is the difference between healthy desensitization and unhealthy "bad faith"?

2. "Many of us know 'good' people who spend long hours on the job, then when they're at home are always fixing something around the house or building something in the basement. Or they're out shopping. They seem addicted to activity" (p. 91). Do you know anyone like that? Does this person seem to have "bad faith" in the sense of this chapter? Why is the person always so busy? What would be a constructive alternative?

3. "A fundamental truth about ourselves is that we are a mixed collection of good and bad components. In Charny's words, 'Human beings are at one and the same time beautiful, generous, creative creatures and deadly genociders'" (p. 94). Can you imagine people you know, live with, work with, becoming "deadly genociders"? What would it take to push them to that extreme?

4. "Good faith does not come by wishing. It must be created, striven for, worked toward" (p. 95). How might one go about working toward good faith?

## Chapter Eight: The Gift of Compassion

1. "Rescuers, like most of the perpetrators, cooperators, and spectators,

were themselves ordinary people" (p. 102). In a time of social catastrophe, in which of these categories would you likely be found? Why?

2. "One doesn't have to be a Thomas Merton or Mother Teresa to come alive with compassion. Everyone is capable of it" (p. 105). How might parents enhance their children's ability to be compassionate?

3. "A third major obstacle to compassion is the incessant stress that presses in on far too many and that seems to be escalating endlessly" (p. 109). How can stress be managed creatively? How do you manage it?

4. "We have entered the era of what Lifton and Markusan called 'species consciousness.' . . . Gandhi had anticipated it much earlier: 'My goal is friendship with the whole world'" (p. 110). Do you think "species consciousness" is possible for most people, or is it the privilege of a few? How might one go about reaching a degree of it?

## Chapter Nine: Good People Doing Good Things

1. "The social activist or civic do-gooder who neglects family or neighbors in the interests of the Big Picture, who is constantly focusing on the horizon and doesn't see the ground directly below, may in fact be avoiding something personally difficult" (pp. 113-114). Do you know anyone like that? How is it possible to do both: concentrate on the people closest at hand, and also be a social activist?

2. List some organizations you know that provide direct help to people, like Hale House (p. 114), the Center of Unity (pp. 114-115), and the Metropolitan Inter-Faith Association (pp. 118 ff.). Why are they effective?

3. List some organizations you know that work for structural change, like the United Farm Workers (pp. 117-118), the Nuclear-Free Philippines Coalition (p. 118), or the Mid-South Peace and Justice Center (pp. 121 ff.).

4. Good people who want to do good things can become involved in direct help and/or in structural change. What factors would be important in deciding how to direct your own compassionate efforts?

## Chapter Ten: Sowing Nonviolent Seeds

1. "The seeds we're looking at here are seeds of nonviolence. They are alive with the gentle power of Gandhi's *satyagraha*. They are bursting with the persuasive energy of Martin Luther King's soul force. These seeds are rich with reverence for the global ecosystem that nurtures us all" (p. 130). How does one go about acquiring such seeds? How could you acquire them?

2. "Gandhi considered nonviolence to be so congruent with human nature that he called it a law of our being" (p. 131). To what extent do you agree with Gandhi that nonviolence is a law of our being? What are your reasons?

3. "When our nonviolent seeds fall on the generous and creative side of human nature, they find the fertile soil that, miracle-like, produces the many-fold grain" (p. 132). Give some instances in your experience of nonviolent seeds falling on fertile soil and producing positive results.

4. "And there might come a time of rare opportunity to exert significant change: ending a famine, averting a genocide, converting to clean energy. The possibilities are limitless" (p. 137). Imagine some such rare opportunity that might come up in your lifetime. How might you take part in what needs to be done?

"The 1971 Synod of Bishops made a major contribution to Catholic social teaching when it insisted: 'Action on behalf of justice and participation in the transformation of the world fully appear to us as a constitutive dimension of the preaching of the Gospel.' In *Why Good People Do Bad Things* Gerard Vanderhaar moves this moral claim from the abstract world of synod documents to the lives of 'good people' who are trying not to 'do bad things.' I recommend it highly."

Walter F. Sullivan
Bishop of Richmond
Bishop-President, Pax Christi USA

"If you're looking for solid, well-written, and accessible material on Christian discipleship issues, Gerard Vanderhaar is always a good buy. His newest work, *Why Good People Do Bad Things*, is true to form.

"Vanderhaar is one of those rare individuals who take seriously both the present realities of the world as it is *and* the Gospel-promised reality of the world as it shall be. Where most would hedge on the one (tinged with cynicism) or the other (flavored with utopian fancy), Vanderhaar insists on the realities of both horror and hope. Better yet, he gives examples, tells stories, both public and personal, allowing the reader to self-identity with both sinners and saints."

Ken Sehested
Executive Director
Baptist Peace Fellowship of North America

"A half-century ago the eminent Catholic sociologist Paul Hanly Furfey shook the religious and academic worlds by tracing the entire complex of social problems to 'the Mystery of Iniquity' [which] 'acts socially through the agency of human groups.' Vanderhaar avoids Furfey's moralistic intensity and more narrow denominational perspective, but his category of evils (economic exploitation, racial injustice, rampant nationalism, etc.) are virtually the same. It all began, of course, with Cain's mocking challenge at the dawn of biblical history. And, as Vanderhaar demonstrates, we may be certain it will continue into the future unless and until 'good' people give the correct answer to Cain's question."

Gordon C. Zahn
Professor Emeritus in Sociology
University of Massachusetts

"There probably could not really be a better work to help the average concerned reader begin to understand 'why good people do bad things.' The explanation of the inner and outer forces is clear, the tone is hopeful, and the underlying faith is apparent. What I suspect will happen is that the reader will be left wanting more. We need to know how to build, in the words of Peter Maurin, 'the kind of society where it is easier to be good.' And it is people like Gerard Vanderhaar who have the resources to help us get a practical vision of 'what the Kingdom of God is like.'"

Dr. Joseph Torma
Institute for Justice and Peace
Walsh University, Canton, Ohio

# GERARD VANDERHAAR

# Why GOOD People Do BAD Things

TWENTY-THIRD PUBLICATIONS
Mystic, Connecticut 06355

## Acknowledgments

Special thanks to Neil Kluepfel, Publisher, for suggesting I do
another book for Twenty-Third Publications, and for his encouraging response to drafts of this one. Thanks also to two of my
colleagues at Christian Brothers University: Dr. Wayne Denton,
Librarian, for his sympathetic understanding and helpful research leads, and Dr. Margaret Miller, Dean of the School of
Arts, for tolerating a teaching schedule that gave me time to
work on the book.

I am indebted to Rev. Paul Brown, faithful worker in the
Memphis vineyard, for his insights into words in worship, and
to Dr. Joseph Catalano, Sartrean scholar, friend of four decades,
and my source for ideas about bad faith and good faith. Once
more I appreciated the skillful wordsmithing of John van
Bemmel, my editor for four books at Twenty-Third.

Finally, in a category by herself, I am grateful to my wife
Janice, whose clear eye and down-to-earth intuition have been
invaluable in this project and just about every other one I have
undertaken in the last twenty-five years.

Twenty-Third Publications
185 Willow Street
P.O. Box 180
Mystic, CT 06355
(203) 536-2611
800-321-0411

ISBN 0-89622-571-2
Library of Congress Catalog Card Number 93-60403

To the dedicated and hard-working staffs of Pax Christi-USA,
the Metropolitan Inter-Faith Association,
and the Mid-South Peace and Justice Center:
good people doing good things.

# CONTENTS

# INTRODUCTION

VIRTUALLY EVERYONE who reads this book would consider himself or herself a "good" person. By "good" I mean trying to be decent, honest, and hard-working, more or less successful in getting through life. None of us is perfect: We're aware of various shortcomings; we're often too busy to be responsive to someone who needs our help; we get upset by the frustrations we face in our jobs; we cut corners here and there; and we probably fudge a little on our income tax. These may be faults or failings, but they're not the "bad things" this book is about.

It's about something less obvious, less direct. It's about that elusive and still not very well understood reality known as our social environment. It's about finding out that the company we work for runs a cheap-labor subsidiary in Mexico and pays workers less than a dollar an hour with no benefits, workers who live in squalor. It's about becoming aware that our church congregation excludes people of another color or sexual orientation. It's about realizing that much of our tax money goes to producing weapons of mass destruction, arming dictators, and training foreign troops who torture suspects and murder dissenters. It's about saving enough money to buy stocks, then learning that some of the best performing corporations are among the worst polluters.

We may likely not know about the misery our investments or our company or our country are causing. Many "good" people are so caught up in the challenges of day-to-day existence that they don't see the broader picture; they are not tuned in to the social implications of their lives and careers. Or they do see it but try to ignore it, because they don't know a way out.

*Why Good People Do Bad Things* attempts to shed light on this troubling ethical quandary. It's written out of the conviction that people of generally good will, reasonably well-balanced, can take a fresh look at the world around them, see its potential as well as its defects in a new way, and determine to be part of the solution rather than part of the problem. At heart, this is an optimistic book.

As more and more of us face up to the realities of our world and come to see some of the things that need to be changed on a broad scale, we can definitely make a difference. But first it's imperative to know what's happening, to see why so many really good people get involved in so many really bad things. Chapter One, "Who We Good People Are," describes us. Chapter Two, "Those We Hurt," gives a sampling of some of the "bad things" people like us become involved in. Chapters Three to Six suggest some powerful currents propelling us toward these bad things. The last four chapters explore alternative visions and opportunities. Each chapter begins with two vignettes that root the chapter in real life experiences.

This book is ultimately about things we can do. It's not a blueprint for solving social problems; it's not the Great Answer for a better world. Great Answers come and go, and most prove to be not so great, at that. But all of us can make some improvements in our own social environment: we can try to lessen the level of violence around us; We can be alert to people who are hurting, perhaps in ways we haven't considered before; and we can join with other like-minded people to try to alleviate some of the hurt.

*Let us endeavor so to live that when we come to die even the undertaker will be sorry.*

—Mark Twain

# CHAPTER ONE

# WHO WE GOOD PEOPLE ARE

"Most of us [CIA paramilitary officers] were bright-eyed and bushy-tailed and displayed all the enthusiasm expressed by the term 'gung ho!' We were young, well-conditioned, eager, caught up in the mystique—of just what we were not quite sure, but we were ready and willing to learn and give it our best....Our group was trained in all aspects of working in and with local resistance movements: parachuting, clandestine radio communications, map reading, survival, explosives, escape and evasion, small unit tactics, and the genteel art of killing silently."[1]

"The Triumphant Individual takes many forms, depending on the prevailing economic winds. The late nineteenth-century version appeared in Horatio Alger's novels about a plucky young fellow who succeeds through hard work, a brave heart, cheerfulness, thrift, discipline, and often a lucky break which is understood to be the reward for all his uncomplaining industry. At his height he rises to the level of a captain of industry, either an empire builder or a robber baron."[2]


WE ARE NOT DISCUSSING in these pages people who knowingly and deliberately do bad things. This book is not about rapists, torturers, extortionists, or child abusers; it's about ordinary people like ourselves. We're not perfect, we have our faults. For the most part we're fortunate enough to have jobs, we pay our taxes, we find time for volunteer work, and we're generally liked by those who know us. We look out for the neighbors, try to be loving with our families, are aware of our civic responsibility to be "good." Some would even call us pillars of our communities. We are not professional thieves or contract killers.

Deep down we know that good people make mistakes and succumb to weakness. But most of us have not sold our souls to the devil. We're trying to struggle through life; we grow up, marry, have families, get jobs, sometimes lose them, but try again. We have accidents, get sick, but keep going. We make mistakes, and try to correct them, or at least regret them and apologize.

This book is not about white collar criminals, like a financial wizard who manipulates the securities system to make big money from worthless bonds, a cynical employer who uses undocumented workers at sub-minimum wage, a calculating bank officer who embezzles millions, or a hardened public official who takes bribes from organized crime. Nor is it about people who have to murder in order to stay in business, such as Mafia families in Sicily or drug lords in Colombia.

It's really not about the Hitlers and Stalins and Pol Pots of the world either, or the faceless Argentine generals in the 1970s who ordered suspected "subversives" dropped from helicopters to their deaths, or Ugandan President Idi Amin who had over 300,000 of his Ugandan citizens killed, including some whose flesh he ate at dinner. And it's certainly not about a demented killer like Jeffrey Dahlmer, convicted for murdering 17 men and boys in Milwaukee, who said he was incapable of stopping himself because he felt he was under the control of an evil power and if released from prison would kill again. Many would consider all of these to be "bad" people who deserved swift and severe punishment.

## Who's Who

Whether there really is such a thing as a "bad" person is a philosophical question. A young man in Mississippi, a former high school quarterback, got hooked on drugs while serving in the army. After he got back home he was arrested for eleven felony crimes to support his craving for cocaine. At the end of his trial, when he was sentenced to ten years in prison, he made this statement: "First of all, I'd like the people in Alcorn County to know I'm sorry for the things I've done." He then thanked the police and sheriff's office for arresting him. "I honestly feel like they saved my life," he said. [3]

Was he a bad person? Many believe that human nature is thoroughly corrupt, totally depraved, that of ourselves we can do nothing really good. A Christian version of this position maintains that our only hope is the transforming grace of God. We are evil until we receive the gift of this saving, amazing grace. Since the majority of people are not saved, it's no wonder the world is so rotten. The Idi Amins, drug dealers, and corrupt politicians confirm for them the reality of fundamental depravity. Perhaps the young man in Mississippi was "saved" while he was in jail, and that's why he was able to acknowledge his crimes. But before that, they would maintain, he was certainly bad, because his nature was corrupt.

At the other end of the spectrum is the conviction that human nature is innately good, noble, and decent, that there's no such thing as a truly bad person. Bad things are done, true, but in this assessment the perpetrator is significantly influenced by his or her surroundings, by a dysfunctional family or a perverted society. The Mississippi quarterback, they would say, was a good person who was victimized by a poor childhood and further corrupted by the temptations he found in military life. Once those troublesome conditions were removed, his natural goodness began to flower. When he was taken away from drugs and rehabilitated, he began to recover his original decency. Do that for everyone and this world will be in excellent shape. Through proper education we can learn about our own potential, discern those forces that may hold us back, and master the tools of self-improvement. Knowing this, we can avoid dangers to ourselves and change destructive forces around us.

A third position, the one on which this book is based and the one I think most people act on practically, is somewhere between. It's the intuition that human beings are mixed. We have good qualities, humane tendencies, but we're also sinners, we're weak, we're susceptible to being dragged down. The biblical image of original sin, the fall of Adam and Eve, teaches that the human race was created whole and wholesome, but right at the beginning trouble came into the picture as an infection. Original sin means that human beings are wounded, weakened. We are basically good, but shaky, and quite capable of doing bad things. But not to despair. Good but shaky people can also accomplish some remarkably fine things. The human condition is full of both advantages and dangers. My assessment is that the young man in Mississippi was fundamentally good, but capable of succumbing to peer pressure and the lure of drugs. The shock of his arrest and conviction brought him to his senses; once he realized where he was heading, he began to straighten out.

Mass murderers, cold-blooded criminals, and sadistic torturers provide severe tests to this position. We're not going to explore it further here. In this book we're looking at basically good people like ourselves who become entangled in operations that have detrimental effects on others. For example, we may find ourselves contributing to the culture of poverty in our community. My wife Janice and I have a friend with real estate holdings in low-income areas of the city. On the whole he's a humane, considerate person. But he made these investments years ago as a cushion for his retirement. Now he sees them somewhat differently. "I guess you could call me a slum lord," he ruefully admitted, "but at least I'm providing homes for people, and I try to keep my properties in good repair."

Another friend of ours is a dynamic corporate executive, happily married with two lovely daughters. He's a devout churchgoer and lives in a fashionable suburb. The trouble is, he works for a multinational corporation with extensive chemical operations in Latin America. Although his firm has repeatedly been cited for ecological pollution and exploitative labor practices, our friend never mentions these problems to us. Instead, he expresses his frustration with what he sees as unreasonable government regulations that hobble his company's flexibility.

## Transnational Corporations

Over the years Janice and I have met interesting men and women in the Netherlands, England, Japan, and the United States who are employed by companies with operations around the world. They are fine people, bright, witty, sensitive, articulate, competent. Some were too young to have been influenced by the Horatio Alger myth in the quotation at the beginning of the chapter, but others undoubtedly were, or had something like it in their own country. We've come to know and like these people—and have been intrigued by the way they see the world.

Many transnational corporations with operations around the globe, such as General Motors, British Petroleum, Royal Dutch Shell, or Nissan, have annual *earnings* larger than the gross national product of mid-sized countries. They provide jobs in Third World countries—and they also take out natural resources and considerable profits from those countries. They prefer to pay as little as possible for both the raw materials and for the labor. In the interests of profit maximization they typically seek to move whatever operations they can to wherever the cost of production is lower. And in the absence of adequate environmental regulations they contribute to the pollution of air and water and the overall worsening of living conditions. The good people we've met who work for companies like these rarely express any sense of unease about harmful effects their employers are causing. Their talk almost always seems upbeat—about "opportunities," "lower costs," and "the competitive edge."

## The Environment

One of the most appalling sights Janice and I have encountered was approaching the city of Dnepropetrovsk in Ukraine during the International Peace Cruise on the Dnieper River in 1990. The clear blue sky suddenly gave way to a curtain of ugly black and bronze smoke pouring skyward out of a complex of industrial plants. As our ship got closer, we could see two distinct atmospheres: the bright summer sky behind us, and then, as though a line had been drawn down the middle, the ugly smoke-filled haze over the factories. It reminded me of the steel mills of Gary, Indiana, thirty years earlier, before pollution control devices were installed.

That sight brought us face to face with the almost total neglect of environmental protection in the former Soviet Union and much of eastern Europe. And yet we met many people in Ukraine and Russia, good, sincere people who believed raw industrialization was necessary to bring a measure of prosperity, even though it was doing substantial damage to the environment and to the populace.

We had experienced something similar a year earlier in the Philippines, a typical Third World country. The pollution in sub-tropical Manila on a humid day was so bad that we had to breathe through a handkerchief. Its visible source was bus, jeepney, and automobile exhausts, mingled with dense smoke from factories. Although the people we met in the Philippines were wonderful—kind, sensitive, gently energetic, they had many more pressing concerns than the air they were breathing. We felt a distinct sense of physical relief the morning we left the Manila melee.

Despite a much greater awareness in western Europe and the United States, environmental hazards still exist. Modern agriculture uses large quantities of herbicides and pesticides, and modern industry produces toxic by-products. Even where regulations attempt to contain harmful chemicals, large amounts of pollutants continue to be discharged into the rivers and air and ground. The once beautiful blue Danube is now the not-so-beautiful tan Danube near Vienna. And it's an even deeper brown as it flows through Budapest.

Automobiles, despite emission control devices where they are required, spew out vast quantities of pollutants into the air. Automobile exhausts have irreparably damaged the Parthenon in Athens, as they have the Colosseum in Rome. From an approaching plane, the haze over Los Angeles can be seen from many miles away. The descent to New York's LaGuardia airport on a hot summer day passes from the clear skies of Pennsylvania and southern New Jersey through the murky mess over Manhattan. Automobile makers around the world, heavily tied to the oil industry, have been appallingly slow to develop electric, battery-powered cars.

## The Military

Some of the finest men I have ever met were the colonels-training-to-become-generals at the U.S. Army War College outside of Carlisle, Pennsylvania. I spent a week with them in 1975 at the National Security Seminar which capped off their special year of training. Most of the colonels were close to my age. We had gone to high school and college at about the same time, knew the same music, remembered the same football and baseball teams. Janice and I had a great time that week socially. The colonels were friendly, disciplined, confident, and skilled at their professional work. They were exactly the kind of "good" people we would want as next-door neighbors.[4]

Except that their professional work was troubling. They were managing different functions of the United States military machine. And that machine at the time we were there was fresh out of the killing fields and skies of Vietnam. It possessed vast quantities of lethal weaponry, from nerve gas to napalm, from anti-tank missiles to anti-personnel bomblets. The military also had hands-on control of the U.S. nuclear arsenal, positioned as a deterrent to what was then the Soviet Union. The Army specifically was responsible for the tactical nuclear shells, mines, and missiles that were ready for use on battlefields around the world.

The U.S. military at the time had an estimated 375 major bases in over 35 countries, with half a million personnel stationed outside the United States, bringing with them the attendant problems of illegitimate children and sexually-transmitted diseases. In the Philippines, Janice and I learned that over half of all the known cases of AIDS in that entire country were women working in towns adjacent to the two largest U.S. military installations, Olongapo next to Subic Bay, and Angeles outside of Clark Air Force Base. When the United States pulled out of those bases in 1992 it left a tragic legacy to the people of the Philippines. And yet the Navy and Air Force personnel who were stationed there or had come for rest and recreation were decent, "good" men and women fulfilling their military commitment.

Some of the colonels we met at the Army War College went on to do a stint at the Pentagon, where they became familiar with the multi-billion dollar defense budget. U.S. military expenditures increased every year from the late 1940s until the Cold War ended—and even then their decline was almost imperceptible. Before the Nixon administration's bookkeeping sleight-of-hand in lumping together all federal income, in-

cluding trust funds and Social Security, it was easy to see that
over half of our tax dollars went to pay for wars past, present,
and future. The Nixon people's public relations trick obscured
that striking statistic. Subsequent national administrations have
found it expedient to keep it obscure.

Government expenditures to meet social needs have been
woefully inadequate by contrast. On a Circle Line boat cruise
around Manhattan, Janice and I saw a tableau that represented
this imbalance. Near our departure dock at 42nd Street was the
large aircraft carrier Intrepid, now a permanent military museum.
Its flight deck showed off sleek Navy and Air Force warplanes.
Next to the Intrepid an abandoned dock had been taken over by
some of New York City's homeless. From their makeshift shelters of cardboard and plastic they waved to us only yards away
from the huge grey hull of the warship, built at a cost of many
millions of dollars—and hundreds of homes. We felt a sad shock
of recognition at this symbol of distorted national priorities.

## Weapons of Mass Destruction

The high military and civilian officials who direct the
country's defense program would certainly be counted among
the good people of the world. But once immersed in the intricacies of the defense system, most of them succumb to the
pressures of maintaining and expanding it, despite evidence in-
dicating it should be curtailed. When Jimmy Carter became
president in 1977, he seemed determined to lower the threat of
nuclear annihilation of which as a former nuclear submarine officer he was well aware. He pledged in his inaugural address to
take steps to banish nuclear weapons from the world. At the
time, the United States had almost 30,000 nuclear warheads of
all sizes and destructive power. The Soviet Union had about
20,000. Both superpowers had thousands of strategic nuclear
missiles aimed at each other, and many thousands more short-
range nuclear missiles and artillery shells intended for battlefield
use. These had been carefully designed, built, and integrated

into battle plans for every conceivable contingency. A whole co-terie of highly specialized military and civilian personnel had been trained in the intricacies of force options and use strategies.

When the newly-elected Carter and his top advisors met with the Joint Chiefs of Staff for the first time, the President posed a question that had been asked by many people outside of government. Why couldn't the United States maintain an ad-equate strategic deterrent with a force of two hundred missiles rather than two thousand? Experts had testified that this lower number was enough to destroy the Soviet Union in a raging hol-ocaust. The generals and admirals around the table were stunned that the President appeared so unsophisticated. Carter's advisors were profoundly embarrassed at what they considered his na-ivete about the U.S. nuclear posture. They quickly set about ed-ucating him on the military, economic, and political need to keep everything in the nuclear inventory, and continue to make more. President Carter never again raised that question pub-licly.[5] Subsequently during his term in the White House, not only were the numbers of nuclear weapons not decreased, but the Strategic Arms Limitation Treaty he signed with Soviet Premier Leonid Brezhnev actually increased the number to which both sides could build.

Most of the men and women who became deeply involved in any aspect of the nuclear arsenal—research, design, pro-duction, transportation, deployment—learned to live with the realization that these weapons would in fact massacre many mil-lions of innocent citizens if unleashed in a war. And the vast majority of these men and women were demonstrably "good" people. Few Dr. Strangeloves were in their number.

A former colleague of mine, a mechanical engineering pro-fessor, was the epitome of a straight arrow. He was good looking, intelligent, a fine teacher, happily married with a growing fami-ly, the very model of a "good" person. He left our faculty to take a position at the Los Alamos National Laboratory, to work in nuclear weapons research and development. Although his colleagues appreciated what the increase in income meant for his family, those of us who were aware of what went on at Los Alamos were sad that someone we knew and liked would choose to contribute his professional expertise there.

In their book *The Genocidal Mentality*, Robert Jay Lifton and Eric Markusan identified some of the coping mechanisms or rationalizations that scientists and engineers at Los Alamos used so they could continue to work on the instruments of death. The most common, they found, was

> the strong conviction, shared with their fellow Americans, that their nation is good, very special, even blessed. They could readily extend that American mythology to questions of technology, making it impossible to believe that America could build a bad machine.[6]

As one of the staff there put it, "Our work at Los Alamos was strongly encouraged by the President of the United States, the Congress, the entire military establishment, and most of the general public." How could anything so approved be reprehensible? The "good" people at Los Alamos continued to develop ever more awesome weapons that threatened the destruction of humankind.

## The CIA

Another legion of "good" people who all too frequently become part of morally repugnant operations work in one or another division of the legendary Central Intelligence Agency. Former officer Ralph McGehee, in the quotation at the beginning of the chapter, described the bright, shiny, squeaky-clean image possessed by the people he met at the agency's headquarters in Langley, Virginia.

One feature of the National Security Seminar I attended at the Army War College was a briefing on the state of the world by the Director of the CIA, who at that time was William Colby. I watched with a mixture of awe and amusement as his helicopter clattered onto the landing circle outside the auditorium minutes before he was scheduled to speak. Out stepped Colby, energetic and alert, followed by several aides with attache cases. He shook hands with the commanding general, then strode inside the auditorium and proceeded to give a 45-minute finely tuned slide lecture on what was going on in the world that the CIA considered important. I was impressed by his smooth lecture technique. But I hadn't quite expected the cavalier attitude he displayed toward the rest of the globe. He spoke patronizingly of Third World countries, as though they didn't really matter very much. And he held the Soviet Union up to ridicule whenever he could. One of his slides was a satellite photo of a Soviet submarine base. The next picture showed the same base but with one of the "submarines" doubled in two. "Obviously a rubber dummy," he said, implying that they couldn't fool us for a minute.

William Colby was, and is now, certainly, a "good" man. Yet a decade earlier he had headed the CIA's infamous Phoenix Program of assassinating village leaders in Vietnam. In the 1970s he came to preside over an agency known for its flagrant disregard of moral norms.[7] Most of the people who worked with him at Langley were equally "good."

## The Arms Trade

I met John F. Welsh, Jr., then Chairman of the Board and Chief Executive Officer of General Electric, at the company's annual shareholders meeting in Memphis in 1984. By virtue of holding a proxy vote of a single share of GE stock owned by the Interfaith Center on Corporate Responsibility, I was admitted to the hotel ballroom where the meeting took place. There I mingled with several hundred genial, affluent men and women, all in good spirits. Although I had dressed for the occasion with suit and tie to look like the rest of the "good" people there, I knew they would consider my mission subversive. Well into the meeting I rose and gave a five-minute talk seconding ICCR's resolution that GE get out of the nuclear weapons business. Heads turned in curiosity. A stony silence greeted my remarks. The Chair then announced that, with all the proxy votes counted, the ICCR resolution was overwhelmingly defeated. The applause that followed was fervent. GE's nuclear weapons business was at the time very good for corporation's bottom line.

Through the 1980s, GE was one of the largest weapons producers in the world. It consistently ranked in the top ten defense contractors, year after year. From the jet engines it manufactured for fighters and bombers, the generating plants for warships, the electronic components for guided missiles and battlefield communications, General Electric showed a substantial profit. Its directors were compensated handsomely. Its stockholders appreciated the solid performance of their shares.

Many of GE's weapons components went into fighter-bombers made by Northrop, Lockheed, and General Dynamics and sold to Third World countries. Others went into warships made in Italy and England which ended up in countries such as Libya and Iraq—where they could have been used against the sons and daughters of some of GE's stockholders.

At the close of that meeting I joined other ICCR people, including several religious women, in a conversation with CEO John Welsh. Everyone called him "Jack." He was a delightful person, poised, charming, and witty. He affirmed his reverence for the "good sisters" who had taught him in Catholic schools when he was a boy. He also said he had no intention of getting GE out of any weapons business.

His decision held for the next eight years. Then GE changed its mind. Partly in response to a national boycott of its other products, GE did get out of the nuclear weapons business by selling its aerospace division, the section that manufactured nuclear weapons systems, to the Martin Marietta Corporation—for over $3 billion.

When one looks at the arms trade with peace eyes instead of dollar signs, its detrimental results become apparent. The spread of sophisticated weapons throughout the Third World has distorted many countries' economic development. It has also fostered the ability of strong-arm leaders to dominate and exploit their own people. Many poor countries, largely as a result of the huge amounts of money spent on weapons, have become burdened with unmanageable foreign debts.

With the demise of the Cold War, the excuse that one superpower had to arm a particular country to counteract the other's influence in that part of the world no longer held. The driving force behind arms sales became much more starkly economic. Weapons exports help the producing country's balance of trade. They are touted as a boost to the national economy by supplying jobs at home.

Most of the GE shareholders in the hotel ballroom in Memphis that sunny April day in 1984, I would guess, were not aware either of the harsh effects of the international arms trade nor of GE's role in it. The company's Annual Report that year glossed over the reality. It stated only that

> the Company continued to strengthen its presence in selected high-potential markets....GE remains among the nation's largest diversified exporters of manufactured goods. Led by aircraft engines, power generation equipment and locomotives, the Company's export sales to external customers were $3.6 billion.[8]

Sidestepping its role as a leading arms maker, GE tried to portray itself as a dynamic component of the American entrepreneurial spirit.

> Successfully implementing a strategy to become the world's most competitive enterprise demands a special company culture—one that's strongly cohesive,

fostering a high level of understanding of what General Electric is trying to do and be. We are advancing a culture that has a sense of urgency, that demands the very best and that emphasizes how crucial an individual's contribution can be to the success of our enterprise.[9]

Many "good" people like Jack Welsh serve as Directors of companies like General Electric, and many other "good" people own profitable stock in such companies. They are not aware of—or choose not to think about—the harm their companies are doing to people in other parts of the world. But, in fact, people are severely hurt, and often killed, by some of the products those companies make.

The good people in this chapter are typical of good people everywhere who live decent, normal lives. Yet the work many of them do professionally or the operations they support financially are a disaster for the people who are hurt by them. It helps to take a closer look these victims.

*An ambulance speeds along the streets to take to the emergency room those it hits by chance along the way.*

—Vassily Belov

# CHAPTER TWO

# THOSE WE HURT

"Andrew G. Galef is an art collector, millionaire investor and resident of one of the nation's wealthiest enclaves, Bel Air, California. Andrew Galef never met Mollie James, but a decision he made in 1989 had a profound effect on her life. Galef eliminated Mollie James's job. For more than three decades, Mollie James worked at the Universal Manufacturing Company in Paterson, New Jersey. In the process, she gained a wage of $7.91 an hour, or more than $16,000 a year. On June 30, 1989, MagneTek, Inc., a Galef company that had bought Universal, halted manufacturing in New Jersey—terminating James's job, along with the jobs of 500 others. The manufacturing operation was transferred to Blytheville, Arkansas, where wages were lower, and part of the existing manufacturing operation in Blytheville was moved to Mexico, where the wages were even lower—less than $1.50 an hour."[1]

"'My son was captured. His head was cut off. My other son disappeared three days ago. I don't know where he is. I'm afraid for him.' The wrinkled, gaunt woman, old beyond her years, spoke slowly from deep pain. She was one of several hundred evacuees who had walked more than seventy hot, dusty miles to seek refuge in the pastoral center of the diocese of Bacolod, on the Island of Negros in the Philippines. They were refugees from the village of Sipalay, driven out by an attack of the army who were attempting to wipe out a contingent of guerrilla fighters. The military called the attack 'Operation Thunderbolt.'"[2]

GANDHI WAS CONVINCED that a person cannot go through a single day without inflicting some pain. Whether we intend it or not, we will hurt other living things, perhaps animal, often human. Some of it is inadvertent—a careless word that wounds, or an accident that injures. Some of it is the by-product of an otherwise good act, like a surgical operation, or disciplining a child. "We are helpless mortals caught in the conflagration of *himsa*," Gandhi wrote. We cannot live "without consciously or unconsciously committing outward *himsa*."[3] It may be unavoidable, like when we instinctively swerve to miss a child running into the street and hit a car in the next lane. Other times we know what we're doing, but feel caught between a rock and a hard place. We make a decision that has unfortunate consequences in order to avoid greater trouble. The manager of a poultry processing plant in North Carolina ordered the fire exits inside the plant locked. Even though it was against fire regulations, he wanted to save fuel and he also wanted to curtail theft by employees. A fire broke out inside the plant, and

25 of those employees died when they couldn't escape through the fire exits. After an investigation, charges were brought against the manager. He pleaded guilty to involuntary manslaughter, and was sentenced to 20 years in prison.[4]

The bad things I want to focus on in this chapter are not inadvertent accidents, which are frequent enough and regretfully familiar in the lives of most good people. Nor will we now be examining the conscious reasoning and subconscious motivation of those who make an unpleasant choice of the lesser of two evils. Later chapters will shed some light on these. Here we are concerned with victims. Many of them are for all practical purposes invisible to the good people causing their plight. They live in faraway lands, have no impact on the mainstream media, but their suffering is real. And it can be traced to decisions made by "good" people sometimes thousands of miles away. These decisions may be perfectly legal and even publicly praiseworthy. They may be initiated with good intentions, aimed at producing good effects—but with distressing results.

## Electricity for Aluminum

Ghana is a poor country of 15 million people in west Africa. It gained independence from Great Britain in 1957. A few years later its new government obtained a large loan from the World Bank to build a major dam on the Volta River. The dam, called Akosombo, was an engineering feat touted as the pride of the new Ghana and a symbol of its modernization. Its purpose, the government said, was to supply hydroelectric power for much of the country.

Ghana is rich in bauxite, the ore from which aluminum is produced. In the early 1960s two multinational corporations, Kaiser and Reynolds, moved into Ghana and formed the Volta Aluminum Company, known from its acronym as Valco. They contracted with the government of Ghana to be exclusive users of the electric power generated by the Akosombo dam. They would pay the government $50 million a year. This was an attractive sum for the new emerging country, but it turned out to be one of the lowest rates for electricity in the world for the amount Valco was using.

The dam was a spectacular success for Valco, but dismal and deadly for millions of Ghanians. When the dam was completed, nearly two million acres of land, largely forests, had been flooded, creating the present Volta Lake. New diseases caused by the ecological upheaval devastated thousands of people. More thousands, displaced by the flooding, had to look for new homes, not always successfully, in other areas of the country.

Even more drastic were the long-term results of the deal with Valco. To supply the power needs for the rest of the country the government built other generating plants, which turned out to be unreliable, erratic sources of electricity. Most of these operated on oil, imported at great expense. Although Ghana was receiving $50 million a year from Valco, it was soon spending $180 million a year for oil. The country fell into abysmal debt. To keep up with debt payments, Ghana began to concentrate its agriculture on the export crop of cocoa, instead of on subsistence farming for its own food needs. It also invited other foreign-owned industries to mine for minerals. This created the need for more electric power, which meant more oil imports—and more debt. Losses to the country from disease, pollution, hunger, and foreign debt were reliably estimated at several hundred million dollars a year. The cost in human suffering could not be estimated.[5] More than three decades after independence, Ghana was a very poor country. Its citizens' life expectancy was 54, ranking it 101st among all the nations. At the same time its energy consumption, still dominated by aluminum, was the 35th highest in the world.[6]

## Moving to Mexico

Ciudad Juarez, across the Rio Grande from El Paso, Texas, is unofficially the second largest city in Mexico. Its real population is uncounted and unknown, because Mexicans by the thousands come and go. Juarez is one of the cities in the *maquiladora* belt of over 2000 factories that have sprung up since the 1970s just south of the border. They extend from Matamoros in the east to Tiujana, a stone's throw from San Diego in the west. Most of these are U.S. companies that have either relocated to Mexico or started there to provide goods and services for the United States. They were attracted by new duty-free provisions on both sides of the border. They were also attracted especially by the low wages of Mexican workers and the lack of environmental protection regulations by the Mexican government. One American visitor described the scene:

> The *maquiladora* factories, notwithstanding their handsome stucco facades and landscaped parking lots, are the modern equivalent of the "sweatshops" that once scandalized American cities. The employers are driven by the same economic incentives, and the Mexican workers in Ciudad Juarez are just as defenseless. The Juarez slums reminded me of the squalid "coal camps" I saw years before in the mountains of Eastern Kentucky.[7]

Multitudes of Mexicans come from the interior in search of the new "American jobs" in places like Juarez across from Texas and Nogales across from Arizona. Despite working for some of the world's most successful corporations—General Electric, Ford, General Motors, GTE Sylvania, RCA, Westinghouse, Honeywell—these men and women, and the many children who also work, are paid as little as 55¢ an hour, hardly a living wage even by Mexican standards.

The *maquiladora* companies pay no property taxes. So Juarez is unable to supply roads, sewers, running water, and electricity, not to mention housing, for the thousands of impoverished families who stream into town hoping to get work in one of the gleaming shops. If they do manage to be hired for a pittance, most have to scrounge pieces of wood or plastic to build shelters on the growing hillside slums outside of town. When they become sick or lose their jobs, they try to either make do in the squalid surroundings or pack up and head back to their original homes.

Moving to Mexico causes casualties among North American workers, too. Many American companies, looking to improve their bottom line, have not hesitated to shut down in New York or New Jersey or Arkansas and set up operations further south. Nearly a thousand employees in a Smith-Corona plant in Corning, New York, lost their jobs when the company moved its typewriter assembly operation to Mexico in 1992. Since Corning's population was only 20,000 at the time, the town was devastated. The job loss affected one-fifth of Corning's families.

Defenders of such moves claim it is a necessity if they want to stay competitive in a global economy. That's the way Andrew Galef saw it in the quote at the beginning of the chapter. And that's why Mollie James in New Jersey, and a fifth of the work force in Corning, New York, lost their jobs. In a further irony, many Mexicans who were initially happy to see the arrival of "American jobs" lose those jobs when their company closes its operations in Mexico and moves to Asia—where wages are even lower.

## Tale of the Tigers

Across the Pacific the large numbers of people in crowded Asian cities provide an abundance of workers for both local and foreign manufacturers. Japanese and American electronic assembly operations in particular have found women in many of these cities to be ideally suited for the patient, intricate tasks needed to assemble computers and video cassette recorders. The same features of low wages, social unconcern, and environmental neglect that made Mexico attractive also characterize these operations in Asia.

I can't forget the vivid description by a young man from

Thailand at an international conference I attended in Belgium. He described how clothing factories in Bangkok routinely employed children to operate the manufacturing machinery. The equipment was small, designed especially for these little ones. When a child slipped and got a hand or foot caught in the works, the injured boy or girl was simply carried out of the factory and laid on the sidewalk. The parents might come along later and find the child. Or they might not. The company was well aware that a multitude of other children was available to take the place of the ones who got hurt.

Four countries—Singapore, Taiwan, Hong Kong, and South Korea—have risen above the rest of their Third World counterparts in industrial productivity. Called the Four Asian Tigers in the economic jargon of fashion, they have been acclaimed as models of what other developing nations can achieve. The largest companies in these countries are highly centralized and carefully subsidized by their governments. Ties with Japan and the West are painstakingly cultivated. One South Korean company, Daewoo, produces a sophisticated line of automobiles and sells them to the Pontiac division of General Motors. For decades, a strong anti-communist atmosphere provided a rationale for labor discipline in these countries. South Korea in particular showed great disregard for worker safety. The International Labor Organization reported that South Korea's rate of 2.26 percent of its workers sustaining serious injury or death annually was the highest in the world. Efforts at organizing workers were quickly repressed not only to ensure uninterrupted productivity, but because the government was concerned that they would provide an opportunity for political unrest.

South Korea became known for its *Kusadae*, the "save-the-company corps." These were gangs of thugs who, at the rise of union rumors, would come into factories and beat up or otherwise intimidate workers. One Korean subsidiary of the Tandy Corporation, maker of Radio Shack products, called in the

Kusadae in 1988. The strong-armed intruders assisted the managers of the plant in a brutal assault on women who were identified as union leaders. Several women were hung upside down and beaten. Others were sexually molested.[8] Through tactics like these, Tandy was able to keep labor costs low and Radio Shack products stayed competitive in the global market.

## The Agony of Arms

Some victims are wounded and killed by the pressures of an inhumane economy. Others, like the refugees in the Philippines described in this chapter's second quote, suffer from the tactics of a tunnel-vision military. Guatemala is a glaring example. Unrest over a foreign-dominated economy and gross inequities among its population were met by increasing military repression. In the 1980s, over 300 companies with ties to the United States were doing business there. They included Goodyear, Coca-Cola, Colgate Palmolive, Philip Morris, Warner Lambert, American Standard, United Brands, U.S. Steel, and Weyerhauser. Bank of America was the largest supplier of funds for agricultural interests. Del Monte, owned by R.J. Reynolds, was the largest U.S. landholder and agricultural producer in the country.[9] These business operations benefitted U.S. stockholders and a small minority of wealthy Guatemalans, but the economic conditions of the vast majority of people steadily worsened.

In the early 1990s, the Guatemalan government intensified its efforts to squelch incipient political opposition. One typical instance occurred on October 10, 1991, reported by Witness for Peace volunteers:

> The Guatemalan military strafed the village of Cabá with machine-gun fire....Residents [said] that they had been fired on for 15 minutes from a military helicopter and an airplane....President Jorge Serrano [said] that the attack was not directed toward any village or civilian population, but rather was "a response

to a group of insurgents." [Other Guatemalans] rejected his explanation, saying, "That is the pretext that they have used to attack us for the last 10 years."[10]

This military operation was typical of tactics used by government forces: sudden raids on villages suspected of harboring insurgents, partly to hunt and kill the rebels, partly to intimidate the villagers.

Military officers from Guatemala and other Third World countries received training in these tactics at the U.S. Army School of the Americas in Ft. Benning, Georgia. The number of Guatemalan military officers in training at the School of the Americas rose dramatically from 12 in 1991 to 312 in 1992. At Ft. Benning, the international training included elements of the stabilization strategy known as "low intensity conflict." It is called low intensity primarily because it does not involve U.S. military in a high-profile role in suppressing unrest in these countries. But it's very high intensity to those who are killed or made to "disappear" because of it.

Operation Thunderbolt, whose aftermath Janice and I witnessed in the Philippines, was an exercise in low intensity conflict. This strategy, in the Philippines, Guatemala, and elsewhere, has been defined by our military as "total war at the grassroots level." It involves extensive civilian defense and intelligence networks, heavy use of propaganda, and the fostering of right-wing organizations. On a military level it includes food blockades and heavy air or ground strikes. It is accompanied by a show of conspicuous but minor improvements by the government—like trumpeted "free" elections between candidates chosen by the elite in the country and endorsed by interested outside powers.

The armaments used in low-intensity conflict are manufactured in the developed countries and sold to Third World governments intent on repressing their own people. Innocent villagers are hurt when their homes are bombed or shelled by weapons supplied by industrialized nations. Guatemalans have been killed by weapons made in many places. Witness for Peace reported a typical instance:

> Three indigenous men and a nine-year old boy were killed by a group of armed men wearing military uniforms at 1:40 am on January 17, [1992] in the settlement named Ciudad Peronia, just south of Guatemala City....According to family members and neighbors, the assailants kicked in the door and spoke with the men before firing on them. Later, police collected 117 cartridge casings scattered near the door. Police said the casings were from a "Galil" automatic weapon, of Israeli manufacture, a model used by the Guatemalan Army.[11]

Weapons manufactured in Israel, the United States, Russia, Belgium, and elsewhere are provided generously when policy or prices dictate. These weapons have devastating effects. An estimated sixty Cambodians a month have been killed or severely wounded by land mines left in their country since the 1960s. Many Vietnamese and Laotians suffered the same fate. More recently, Kuwaitis have fallen victim to the several million mines laid by Iraqi solders during their short-lived incursion in 1991.

Land mines come from many places. Companies in Spain, Italy, and Greece manufactured a lightweight, 5-ounce version that could be strewn by helicopter or buried by hand. The former Soviet Union marketed a land mine that weighed six pounds. When stepped on, the mine jumped five feet in the air and sent jagged metal pieces into whatever bodies were nearby. The international arms trade is big money to weapons producers. The countries that buy them, usually poor to begin with, increase their international debt in order to finance the purchases.

Their people are doubly hurt—by the weapons themselves, and by the resulting economic deterioration that increases their misery.

## Foreign Debt

Brazil is one country burdened by a huge debt to foreign banks. A Pax Christi International delegation, visiting Brazil in the late 1980s to assess its social and economic climate, reported: "Everything in the country is seen, evaluated, programmed and decided under the dark threat of interest to be duly paid, with no means to stop the financial bleeding that is leading the country to a breakdown."[12] The debt affected patterns of land use in Brazil, as agriculture in the familiar shift came to be viewed primarily as a source of foreign exchange and less as food for internal consumption. Emphasis was given to large-scale commercial farming and to export crops. Malnutrition began to increase among poor Brazilians, whose average calorie consumption dropped to 200 fewer than the daily minimum requirement. The mechanization of agriculture resulted in more unemployed, more poor, many of whom flocked to the cities in an effort to find work and stay alive. As a consequence of these population shifts, more and more homeless children plagued the cities with criminal activities. Reports began to appear about urban hunters who searched out homeless children and killed them for bounty. Both hunter and hunted became wretched victims of economic dislocation fueled by foreign debt.

Beleaguered nations have been pressured to insure, as far as possible, that they continue to pay at least the interest on what they owe. When I visited Cuba in 1986, Fidel Castro, in his provocative way of going to the heart of the matter, had issued a call to Third World countries to close their books on all debt owed the First World. Wipe the slate clean, he said. The interest you have already paid is greater than the amount of the loans in the first place. His call was heard but not heeded. Significant diplomatic and economic pressure was exerted on debtor nations. The entire international financial system was said to be at stake.

Poor nations have generally acquiesced when international lending agencies imposed the strict terms known as Economic Structural Adjustment Programs, or ESAP. The government of Kenya, for instance, was required to provide irrigation for export crops of coffee, cotton, and pineapples—but was unable to do the same for crops grown for food for its own people. Zimbabwe was forced to begin planting tobacco for export on fields that had been used for growing maize. A man waiting in a food line in Harare was asked if he knew about ESAP. "Oh yes," he said. "That stands for Ever Suffering African People."[13]

The amount of international debt owed by Third World countries in the early 1990s was in the one trillion dollar range. Most of it simply could not be repaid, and never would be. Poor countries trying to keep up with just the interest payments were forced to abandon whatever efforts they might have made to halt ecological deterioration. That was a luxury far beyond their means. As a consequence, many have experienced serious environmental problems as their timber and mineral resources are exhausted. According to a 1989 report by UNICEF:

> At least half a million young children have died in the last twelve months as a result of the slowing down or the reversal of progress in the developing world...which is the result of unprecedented borrowing, rising interest rates, falling commodity prices, inadequate investment of borrowed funds, and the domestic and international management of resulting debt crisis.[14]

Julius Nyerere, the former president of Tanzania, put the problem starkly: "Must we starve our children to pay our debts?" Many "good" people would cringe at having to give an affirmative answer to his question. But put the question another way. Should a country be required to repay what it has borrowed, even if it means belt-tightening of its internal economy? Most "good" people would answer yes without hesitation. They will never hear about the children who starve as a result.

## North American Ills

Most of us are well aware of social ills plaguing the United States. We see them all around us: the gaunt young man holding a cardboard "Will work for food" sign; broken windows and peeling paint at a public housing project; daily reports about drive-by shootings and stabbings in public schools; increasing incidence of bank robberies and bankruptcies. Catalogues of these trends abound. So do analyses of their causes. So, unfortunately, do their victims. I would focus here on only two such problems resulting from the actions of "good" people.

One is birth defects in children born to mothers living near toxic waste sites. It has been statistically demonstrated (in a 1992 study by Yale University and the New York Health Department) that more infants are born with defects to mothers living within a mile of any chemical dump than to mothers living outside that radius. And the number of such infants increased dramatically when their mothers live near sites that are specifically designated as dangerous.

Many "good" people are involved in creating and spreading toxic waste. Disposal of harmful industrial by-products is poorly regulated in the United States. Waste dumping has been going on for a long time. Only recently have its health hazards been demonstrated. To install adequate containment or conversions systems is costly. Operators are reluctant to take on the additional expense. Plants that routinely release harmful chemicals into the air or into a nearby pit, river, or lake are supposed to see that these chemicals are contained, and must report appropriate measurements to the federal government. But the regulations rely largely on self-enforcement, and this is not always strict.

More babies continue to start life with handicaps that will impair their growth and development.

A second issue involves indirect acquiescence rather than direct responsibility. It is the woefully substandard housing for people unable to afford decent accommodations. I was moved by the story of a young woman who took her two children to another city to escape an abusive husband. Her very limited resources allowed her to rent a small apartment which turned out to be infested with roaches and rodents. When she first moved in, she and her children often went hungry because it took a while to negotiate the process of getting food stamps. Finally, she was able to buy enough groceries for a decent meal. When they finished it, her three-year-old boy left the table clutching a piece of cheese. After the weeks of hunger he would not give it up. But as soon as he fell asleep, his mother had to remove it from his fist. She knew that rats would come for the cheese and bite her child during the night. Her meager income did not allow her to provide a safer home for her children. Public resources for helping her live in a rat-free environment were not available.[15]

It has been estimated that the cost of restoring all the public housing units in the United States to a level of decency would cost $20 billion. This amount happens also to be the cost of ten B-2 stealth bombers. Almost everyone would feel sorry for children at risk from rodents. But if they had to make a choice between restoring public housing and producing the B-2 bomber, most "good" people, especially those in government, in the Pentagon, and in the plants that manufacture components for the B-2, would choose the latter. Dozens of Tomahawk cruise missiles were fired at Iraqi targets in and around Baghdad in attacks long after the war was over. Each Tomahawk missile cost 1.3 million dollars. Yet many "good" people applauded the attacks. They would rather see Saddam Hussein humiliated than public housing rehabilitated.

Almost all of us would say we need to have adequate housing for everyone, and we need to prevent as many birth defects as possible. That's our humane sensitivity. That's what we learn in church and in our formal education. Unfortunately, our culture communicates a different message:

—Poor people are lazy.
—Jobs are plentiful, even if they are low-paying.
—It's good to be rich.
—Our country needs a strong, high-tech defense.
—People who live with rats are incompetent.
—Everybody can improve themselves if they work hard.

Life is spotted with hurt. We good people may not be able to go through a single day without perpetrating some *himsa*, as Gandhi acknowledged. But much of the suffering in our world can be avoided; much pain need not be inflicted. "God, give me the patience to accept the things that can't be changed, the courage to change those that can, and the wisdom to know the difference," as a perceptive prayer expressed it. To know what can be changed and what can't calls for discernment, figuring out what's really going on. The discernment involves trying to understand why so many "good" people contribute to all this suffering.

*Goodness must be joined with knowledge. Mere goodness is not of much use, as I have found in my life.*

—Gandhi

CHAPTER THREE

# WHY WE DO THESE THINGS

"Northwest Airlines announced it will lay off more than 1000 workers, including about 80 Memphis-based flight attendants. 'Adverse economic conditions and the brutal economic environment of the U.S. airline industry have required us to take aggressive action to reduce costs and improve operational efficiency,' Northwest's vice president of human resources said. 'We have had to make difficult decisions, and none is more difficult than reducing the workforce. However, we will take the actions necessary to assure Northwest Airlines' long-term prosperity.'"[1]

"All during my trip [in Vietnam] I asked our troops how they felt about the war. Ninety percent gave me roughly the same answer: 'We have to stop

Communism and we'd rather do it here in Vietnam than on the coast of California.' One F-4 fighter-bomber pilot in Danang told me he thought we should start at the DMZ and kill every man, woman and child in North Vietnam."[2]

GOOD PEOPLE ARE not sadistic. We don't delight in causing pain, and yet disturbing forces are at work around us. We often find ourselves implicated in processes where people are hurt. Perhaps we can't control these forces or resist them or extricate ourselves from them.

Or perhaps we can.

But first we have to know them. Here are five imperatives that push good people into positions of hurting others. They stem from technology, economics, the drive for power, from ideology, and even from the urge to be charitable.

## The Technological Imperative

One of the most fundamental characteristics of human beings is our tool-making capacity. The philosopher Henri Bergson wanted to define our species not as *homo sapiens* but as *homo faber*, toolmakers. We make tools because of the combination of our physical limitations and our intellectual creativity. Our hands can only reach a short distance, but our minds can invent ways of reaching around the world. Long ago our ancestors figured out how to use a stick to knock bananas from a tree. They discovered how to control fire for warmth and cooking. They invented the wheel to move large loads. From the very beginning we humans have used our ingenuity to expand our influence and improve the quality of our life. This drive to move, to create, to accomplish is so basic, so pervasive, that it was seen as a divine mandate at the dawn of humanity. In the Bible God told the first humans, "Fill the earth and subdue it. Rule over the fish of the sea and the birds of the air and over every living creature that moves on the ground" (Genesis 1:28).

Since that early dawn we have come from knocking bananas out of trees to producing microwave meals, nutritionally sensitive nouvelle cuisine, and space age food of the future. From an accidental spark of flint and iron, we have invented the internal combustion engine, and climate-controlled living environments. The frontiers of the possible are being pushed back daily. Our culture embodies a strong belief that if it can be built, it should be built. And if it can't be built yet, let's get to work and figure out what it takes to build it tomorrow.

Some decades ago I graduated from Tinker Toys to erector sets. I learned how to make a crystal radio receiver. I could take my bike apart and put it back together in working condition. I can appreciate the attraction video games and personal computers have for today's youngsters. I can appreciate the feeling of sophisticated accomplishment that comes from designing the Saturn car, or shepherding the Magellan spacecraft to Venus.

But the same technological imperative that extended our reach to the stars also spelled trouble on Earth, from the beginning. The stick for knocking bananas out of a tree could also be used as a club for beating someone's brains in. The crude club gave way to the slashing sword. And spears for hunting animals were also useful for hunting enemies. Of course, swords and spears themselves don't kill people, people kill people. But when the swords and spears are there, sharpened and ready, some people are going to kill others with them. Eventually some of our ancestors figured out a more effective way to kill by combining metal with fire, and by discovering gunpowder. Others made bigger and better guns to gain the competitive edge. From guns to hydrogen bombs was but one small step for humankind, albeit one giant step toward humankind's destruction.

The abacus gave way to the adding machine. It wasn't long before computer-generated securities trading made instant fortunes possible. The computer also made possible large-scale fraud like savings-and-loan scandals and international banking scams. From the ox-cart to the automobile, from Kitty Hawk to the Concorde, we humans have figured out ever faster ways of getting where we want to go. But the same generation of aircraft that can carry us to any major city in the world in less than a day can also obliterate every major city in the world on the same day.

Good people, excited by intellectual challenges, have produced greater and greater technological marvels. Too often, though, the excitement of the challenge overcame moral judgment—and the technological marvel they proudly displayed wreaked havoc. The physicists who worked on the Manhattan Project at Los Alamos embarked on a grand adventure of intellectual challenge. Spurred on by the technological imperative, they accepted the challenge. If an atom bomb could be built, it should be built. And they figured out a way to build it. Their creation, the Little Boy that obliterated Hiroshima, thrust the world into the terrors of the Nuclear Age. Good people all, they victimized humanity because they themselves were victimized by the technological imperative, the drive to build and the applause that greeted their ingenious invention.

## The Economic Imperative

Besides the technological imperative's seemingly insatiable drive to push back the frontiers of the possible, good people are subject to the spell of money. Innocent enough in its function of providing for our basic needs, the economic imperative, almost before we know what's happening, can entangle good people in questionable enterprises.

For many of us, the economic imperative started with a simple summer job: cutting grass, bagging groceries, lifeguarding at a swimming pool. For most others in the world, a different kind of work was vital for survival from childhood: laboring long hours in fields or factories to eke out a meager income for food and shelter. Given the pressures in a struggling economy to provide for life's necessities, moral compunction over the kind of work one did seemed to many a luxury they couldn't afford. A sign outside a restaurant in Iuka, Mississippi, when the TVA's Yellow Creek nuclear power plant was under construction there in the late 1970s, proclaimed:

> Nukes pollute us
> with money
> We love it

The health hazards, ecological damage, and intractable disposal problems involved in nuclear energy all paled before the prospect of high-paying jobs in a poor corner of a poor state.

The man fortunate enough to secure a union job in an automobile plant, who works steadily and faithfully for years and finally reaches the plum position of driving the new cars off the assembly line, will probably not resign when he finds out that the cars his company makes have flaws that cause fatal accidents. He needs the job, and values his seniority. The finance graduate who starts off as a junior bank officer and is gradually initiated into the mysteries of investment policies will probably not jeopardize her career by exposing her bank's illegal withholding of loans in low income areas. And her bank's senior officers will try to enhance its profitability by providing loans to an industry that is planning to shut down its local manufacturing line and relocate to Mexico.

A vice president of one company planning just such a move frankly acknowledged the suffering it would entail—but the economic imperative overrode his qualms. "On a local basis, it can be a tragedy. That, we regret," he said. "But to keep our 16,000 people employed, we need to stay in business. We've got to put together the kind of competitive package that can really compete on a world scale."[3] When the interests of the company clash with the interests of the public, the economic imperative will strongly urge favoring the company. "I was asked the other day about United States competitiveness," the president of a multinational corporation proclaimed, "and I replied that I don't think about it at all." His own organization's success far out-weighed his concern for the common good. The same sentiment was voiced by the head of an American company's subsidiary in Taiwan. "The U.S. trade deficit is not the most important thing in my life. Running an effective business is."[4]

The young engineer who is offered a starting salary higher than many of his college professors will probably not resist when his employers assign him to the weapons-design unit of the company. And the directors of that company will be actively promoting those very weapons to any government able to pay for them, regardless of its human rights record. If the armored vehicles and sophisticated aircraft they provide are used to keep a brutal regime in power, that may be regrettable, but it's profitable. The company's public relations staff knows how to package such transactions in terms of providing jobs and boosting the local economy. In the spring of 1992, the CEOs of six major weapons corporations sent a letter to the President of the United States urging him to approve the sale of 72 F-15 fighter planes to Saudi Arabia. They claimed that the project "would rapidly inject $5 billion into the economy...at no cost to the U.S. taxpayer."

The economic imperative also drives the news and entertainment media, which in turn have great influence over the values and attitudes of so many good people. Although we may profess to accept the values communicated in church or school, we are often exposed to powerful, contradictory ones when we go to a movie or turn on the television. We may really believe that we should love our neighbor, but an incessant message in the media is to exploit the neighbor. Television programs and movies featuring violence and affluence appeal to viewers. Large audiences attract advertisers and sponsors, and this, in turn, enables similar programs to be shown and similar movies to be made. The cycle is vicious; its effects are corrosive: More neighbors are exploited.

The sports editor of the Memphis daily newspaper lamented the need to run a story about a tennis star who contracted AIDS through a blood transfusion. The editor admitted that the paper had to pander to what is less noble in its readers.

> I wish it were otherwise—and I'm not alone. Most reputable reporters would prefer to exercise more discretion, more compassion in covering the news. But the public's appetite for details and the competitive nature of the business often conspire to make callousness a job requirement.[5]

Besides the micro-economic imperative of making a living for oneself and enhancing the profits of one's company, we in the West live under the macro-economic imperative of the capitalist system of production and consumption. Most of those who benefit from this system never seriously look at its harmful side-effects:

1. Historically, capitalism was built on the backs of the oppressed: slaves, colonies, natural resources seized from other lands.

2. It demands a certain level of unemployment, and therefore poverty, in order to work right.

3. Because its driving force is personal profit, it fosters an attitude of greed, taking for oneself at the expense of others.

4. When unregulated, it results in great wealth for a few and poverty for most others, as in the age of the moguls in the United States, and in the early years after the collapse of communism in the former Soviet Union and eastern Europe. Too often we see the few wealthy and powerful using forces of repression against the many poor.

The economic imperative—micro and macro—constitutes such a given that most good people don't even think about the possibility of living apart from it. Like the weather, we talk about it, complain when inflation is high or employment low, but most of us will unfurl the umbrella and trudge doggedly ahead through the rain. The economic imperative is taken for granted. It's responsible for good people doing many bad things.

# The Power Imperative

In addition to the mixed mechanical blessings of the technological imperative and the desire for money at the root of the economic imperative, another force driving good people to do bad things is the attraction of power. The ability to control our surroundings, to make others conform to our wishes, is deep and can be deadly. National power, backed by technological proficiency, is extremely dangerous. In an earlier age of national naivete, we were brought up to think of our country as right, under God. Our growth from sea to shining sea was seen as Manifest Destiny, not imperialistic expansion. We regretted our centuries of slavery, but softened their cruel exploitation with images such as Stephen Foster penned in his song "My Old Kentucky Home": "The young folks roll on the little cabin floor, all merry, and happy, and bright."

Wars, even the ones our country started against Mexico and Spain, were considered noble crusades, fought to preserve freedom or bring the blessings of democracy to some corner of the world. When the enemy proved intractable, as in Vietnam, many, like the F-4 pilot in the quote at the beginning of this chapter, wanted simply to eliminate them and get the job over with. Most "good" people continued to internalize the historical myths, proud to belong to the most powerful nation in the history of the human race. It makes one feel good to be Number One, to have other nations defer to us, other people long to live like us. Our nation's undisputed power around the world bolsters our own wobbly egos. We hold our head a little higher when our flag flies proudly in Managua or Mogadishu or Moscow.

After Vietnam, the only war our country ever lost, many Americans felt a nagging sense that our power was diminished. The Iran hostage-taking and the failed rescue mission underlined what seemed to be our national impotence. The Soviet invasion of Afghanistan, which we were unable to stop by either overt diplomatic or clandestine military means, was further cause for uneasiness. The quick conquest of Granada brought

momentary relief, but its miniscule achievement caused it to
fade in quiet embarrassment. The invasion of Panama showed
more muscle, but Noriega succumbed meekly in a Miami court-
room, and the drugs continued to flow. Something grander was
needed, and in 1990 it came: the crisis in the Persian Gulf.

For six fervent months, as Desert Shield turned into Desert
Storm, Americans' desire to feel good about their country and its
powerful place in the world was focused not on our democratic
values, not on our humanitarian ideals, not on the physical
beauty of our land, but, as Richard Barnet put it, "on the nation's killing power."[6] It seemed that most of the country was
transformed into a cheering section for the men and women
creating the storm in the desert. Few protested the war. Most
were oblivious to the government's censorship of what was going
on there; something bigger was going on here. Our president had
given us what we needed: We were back on top again. Never
mind the 100,000 or so Iraqi soldiers slaughtered from the air.
Never mind the nearly 200,000 Iraqi children who would die
within months of the war from diseases brought on by the disabled water and sewage systems.[7] We had proven to the world,
and more important, to ourselves, that we were again Number
One.

A month after that war ended came the Pentagon's policy
draft about maintaining our top spot. It minced no words in pro-
claiming that America's political and military mission from now
on was to ensure that no rival superpower would be allowed to
emerge. To stay on top, the policy draft said, the United States
"must sufficiently account for the interests challenging our leadership or seeking to overturn the established political and economic order."[8] Although negative press reaction caused the
draft document to be withdrawn, few doubted that the Pentagon
in this case was speaking for most Americans, under the influence of the power imperative.

Most "good" people feel at ease with our national leaders,
even when we disagree with some of their policies, even when

we admit that they reached their high positions as a result of their own personal power drive. When an obviously cynical manipulation of the internal political system comes to light, like Watergate or the Iran-Contra deception, the power imperative impels us to dismiss it as an aberration. We want our leaders to be right. We identify with the power they possess. This trust level is consciously sustained by Washington's careful cultivation of the media. Richard Barnet pointed out the special success the Reagan administration had in this area. Enormous energy was expended at the highest levels in the White House on the crafting of appearance. The President's closest aides even boasted to reporters how they manipulated the media and the public. They would meet at 8:15 in the morning at the White House to set "the line of the day" so that the White House "spin" would blanket the news. The agenda was usually the same: "What are we going to do today to enhance the image of the President? What do we want the press to cover today and how?"[9] Ronald Reagan became famous as the Teflon President. Criticism did not stick to his genial persona. During the Iran-Contra hearings, Reagan and his advisors correctly felt that the public really didn't want to know the truth. They were able to pass it off as the President's inability to recall, a momentary lapse of memory.

Power in itself is neutral; it can be used for good or ill. Almost everyone wants it. When we don't have enough of it personally, we can satisfy our urge vicariously through identifying with a powerful institution such as our country. But the possession of power can be intoxicating. The desire to use it and retain it can have unfortunate consequences for those who stand in its way. Walter Wink has noted, "Not only does power tend to corrupt, but often it is the most ruthless and corrupt who tend to gain power."[10] John Gardiner, founder of Common Cause, once said that he had never fought any tougher battles than with those who were requested to relinquish some of their power. "I'd been through some rough issues—race and poverty, but I never knew what real slugging was until I got into the ways people in power preserved their power."[11] The desire to have power over others, to bend them to our will, is one of the fundamental drives that lead good people astray from the path of humane behavior.

## The Ideology Imperative

If the unexamined life is not worth living, as Socrates believed, the examined life can become hazardous when it is reinforced by a rigid ideology. The search for meaning leads thinking people to a set of beliefs and ideas about life and the universe. When these beliefs and ideas are systematized and made to fit together in a pattern that not only explains the world but provides a guide for living in it, they make up what is called a worldview, a philosophy of life. It's also called an ideology. Although the word "ideology" often has negative connotations, it basically means a systematic body of concepts about human life and culture, about the world in which we live. Since people usually act according to the way they believe, our philosophy of life, our ideology, provides guidance in the choices we have to make every day. Finding the right ideology is uplifting. It gives meaning and purpose to life.

The problem comes when my philosophy of life, my ideology, calls me to take certain actions, and you're in the way. If my ideology is rigid and what you're doing doesn't fit into it, then I have to get you out of the way. You may have your own ideology that keeps you where you are, but if mine says you have to move, then I'm going to take measures that will make you move. Most ideologies contain visions of what the world should be like. An ideology that is too rigid does not have a place for genuinely different perspectives. In marching toward what my ideology says the world should be like, I may have to force you to conform. Too bad, but it's necessary. If what I'm after is worthy of pursuit, I may not balk at doing whatever it takes to get it, even if some unfortunate side-effects occur. "You can't make an omelet without breaking some eggs," runs conventional wisdom. This wisdom is morally corrupt, though, when the eggs that are broken are people who are hurt.

Crusades of all types are based on rigid ideologies. The European Christians who marched under the banner of the cross to liberate the Holy Land from the Muslim "infidels" were acting out of an ideology that proclaimed God wanted the whole world to accept the one true (i.e., Christian) religion. And those who didn't, who believed another way, had to be forcibly removed if they didn't change. The American troops in Vietnam in the quote at the beginning of this chapter were acting on the basis of an ideology: The American way of life, including democracy and freedom, was the way the world should be. Since the Vietnamese Communists were impeding this way of life, they had to be stopped, and eliminated if necessary. The titanic struggle between competing ideologies known as the Cold War wreaked havoc, material and spiritual, on both sides.

Many ideologies, worldviews, appeal because they are grandiose. They provide a big picture and help me situate myself in a scheme of things that's much larger than my relatively insignificant life. They make me feel like I'm participating in a grand cause. If my ideology contains liberty and justice for all, for everyone in the world, that's noble, that serves the cause of human progress. If another ideology contains freedom from hunger and deprivation, lifting the poorest of the poor into a level of equality with all, that too is noble, that too serves the cause of human progress.

Some ideologies are narrow, prosaic, banal, such as the belief that the purpose of life consists in accumulating wealth. "What are your career plans?" my wife Janice asked a young high school graduate who hadn't yet settled into a steady job. His answer: "I just want to make a lot of money." There it was, stark and clear, some would say the American Dream. He was a decent young man, whose family values would not allow him to rob banks or deal drugs. But other than the obviously illegal, or what was socially unacceptable to his peers, his employment horizon was wide open. Make as much as you can as fast as you can. It doesn't matter who is hurt in the making. So much of our Western media, education, advertising—our cultural milieu—encourages people to buy into this ideology, to want to emulate lifestyles of the rich and famous. They easily support laws that favor the few at the expense of the many. Columnist George Will has observed that "Americans are happiest when pursuing happiness, happiness understood as material advancement."[12]

Some ideologies are actually committed to life-destruction, as was the Nazi super-race belief that inferior peoples must be exterminated. Once joining with others, perhaps not initially realizing the dark dimensions of the ideology, it's hard to extricate oneself. The need for self-esteem, the comradery of colleagues, the team spirit—even in a destructive cause—provide psychic income that's hard to give up. Group experiences can be hypnotic and magnetizing. When people get caught in the grip of a powerful process, they become vulnerable to values that otherwise would not be acceptable to them. Those Germans who adopted the Nazi ideology of establishing a new Reich based on racial purity brought on a conflagration that consumed fifty million lives.

Because ideologies make sense out of life and provide a purpose for living, they are attractive. Because ideologies can be rigidly intolerant of those who stand in their way, they are dangerous. The ideology imperative can tap into our dark side, our ability to be destructive. All of us have within ourselves the capacity to hurt. "Good" people need to be especially alert that the ideology they have accepted as a coherent view of the universe does not tap this capacity, does not propel them into causing hurt.

## The Charity Imperative

Most "good" people have a desire to reach out and help someone. "Good" people are generous. Pillars of society often accept leadership roles in charitable causes. And there is an ample supply of unfortunates who need help. Jesus' words, "The poor you will always have with you" (Matthew 26:11), have been accurate for two thousand years. Good people can always find outlets for their spirit of generosity. In some strange way, though, the imperative of charity may contribute to prolonging the very poverty it seeks to alleviate. It is often easier to reach out and help someone than to change the conditions that make the person need help in the first place. Martin Luther King, preaching on the parable of the Good Samaritan, praised the man who stopped to help the victim of robbers on the road to Jericho. Then he also talked about the need for a Jericho Road Improvement Association.

> It is not enough to aid a wounded man on the Jericho Road; it is also important to change the conditions which make robbery possible. Philanthropy is commendable, but it must not cause the philanthropist to overlook the circumstances of economic injustice which make philanthropy necessary.[13]

Philanthropists, Good Samaritans, generous people reaching out to help, receive due acclaim when their efforts become known. They are respected members of the community, and properly so. Those who work to improve conditions on the Jericho Road, to eliminate robbery on it, or to straighten out the injustice of racism or sexism, are not always equally acclaimed. Mother Teresa, rightly admired for her tireless dedication to the poor, was accepted and loved worldwide. Martin Luther King, who tried to change the system of racial segregation that propagated poverty, was not accepted and loved worldwide. Neither was Daniel Berrigan, the poet priest who would rid the world of nuclear weapons *now*. Dorothy Day, the founder and inspiration of the Catholic Worker movement, was applauded for giving food and shelter to whoever needed it, no questions asked. But the response to Dorothy Day who sat on a picket line with striking farmworkers in California and who refused to pay taxes in New York, was not nearly as enthusiastic. Mother Teresa may well be canonized a saint. Dorothy Day, when it was suggested that she, too, could receive the honor of sainthood, replied, "They can't dismiss me that easily."

Dom Helder Camara, longtime archbishop of Recife in the poor northeast corner of Brazil, said, "When I feed the poor they call me a saint. When I ask why they are poor, they call me a communist!" In one of his last public appearances, at the Pax Christi national assembly in 1992, his stirring words called for "a millennium without misery." For that to happen, for the next millennium to be considerably less miserable than this one, the world needs Good Samaritans who reach out to help victims on the road of life—but it also needs strong hands and valiant hearts to straighten out troublesome parts of that road. Good people have to be alert that the generosity of the first not be a barrier to the hard work of the second. We continue to feed the poor, but we also continue to ask why they are poor—and figure out how to act on the answer.

Our search for answers takes a hard look at social imperatives contributing to misery. It also leads us to some of the roots of those imperatives deep in the human psyche. We need to take a deep breath and shine a light into our own personal Shadow.

*I do not understand my own actions. For I do not do what I want, but I do the very thing I hate.*

—Romans 7:15

CHAPTER FOUR

# THE SHADOW KNOWS

"On March 19, 1988, a silver Volkswagen Passat was [accidentally] driven into a funeral procession on its way from St. Agnes Church to the Milltown Cemetery in Belfast. The dead man, thirty-year-old Kevin Brady, had been killed three days before by a deranged Unionist assassin. The [Passat] driver and his companion, two [British] army corporals not in uniform, were surrounded and trapped by the mourners, pulled out of their vehicle, beaten, stripped of their clothing and thrown over a wall, bundled into a taxi, shot, and abandoned on a piece of waste land."[1]

"The generals and officials were calm and rational throughout the presentations while numbers and strategies were discussed. Several hours later, I stood up and laid out the clinical details of nuclear war in

stark detail. General Daniel Graham, a member of
the Committee on the Present Danger, exploded like
a champagne bottle being uncorked. He was fine as
long as nuclear war was not discussed from a medical
or emotional perspective, but as I explained the clinical details, his dark side erupted and was directed at
me and toward the Soviets."[2]

A POPULAR RADIO DRAMA of the 1940s began each
episode with a low, mysterious voice intoning, "Who knows
what evil lurks in the hearts of men?" After a slight pause came
the answer: "The Shadow knows," followed by a disquieting
laugh. This radio Shadow was an anonymous, secretive character who understood the criminal mind. On the side of law and
order, he foiled a different plot every week.

As we seek to understand why it is that good people often
do bad things, it helps to look at another Shadow, this one cour-
tesy of psychoanalyst Carl Jung. Jung gave the term "shadow" to
the dark unpleasant side of the human psyche. This Shadow is
usually unconscious. We don't avert to it; we're often not even
aware it's there. It consists of traits and tendencies we don't like
in ourselves, such as lust, laziness, self-righteousness, or self-
hatred. Lurking in our Shadow are those secret shortcomings we
refuse to face, or which we uneasily perceive but shove out of
sight because we're ashamed of them. Jung chose the word
"shadow" for this concatenation of characteristics because he believed they often reveal themselves in dreams as a mysterious
person, a shadowy image of the dreamer's conscious self. They
show up as feelings we wouldn't accept in daily living. Or they
take the form of someone leading us into a bizarre experience.
Reflecting on these shadowy dream images, Jung believed, can
yield significant clues to our personality. Like the radio Shadow
who knew the dark secrets of the criminal mind, our own personal Shadow contains many of the dark secrets of our own attitudes and actions.

Most of us would rather not probe our Shadow too deeply; uncomfortable feelings percolate inside us when we admit our troublesome traits. Most of us also don't want to risk losing the approval of family and friends. We assume they will disapprove if they know we are really lustful or lazy or self-righteous or afraid, or whatever else we think they hold in low esteem. So we're inclined to push this unsavory cluster of impulses down and away, try not to think about them, minimize them in our own mind, even repress them from our conscious self-image. Philosopher William Barrett called these unpleasant aspects of ourselves the Furies. They are "hostile forces from which we would escape. And of course the easiest way to escape the Furies, we think, is to deny that they exist."[3]

But denying they exist doesn't really make them go away. Repressing them from awareness can even intensify their presence, turning them into a caldron of witches' brew simmering under the veneer of our rational, civilized behavior. And this witches' brew can be crippling, as Thomas Merton observed:

> As long as we believe that we hate no one, that we are merciful, that we are kind by our very nature, we deceive ourselves; our hatred is merely smoldering under the gray ashes of complacent optimism. We are apparently at peace with everyone because we think we are worthy. That is to say we have lost the capacity to face the question of unworthiness at all.[4]

Precisely because we haven't come to grips with it, our Shadow cluster often shows up in abrupt behaviors that leave us wondering "Why did I do that?" Sudden anger at a child's innocent antics, or an inappropriately severe denouncement of a colleague's mistake can leave us surprised. "I guess I just lost control." Or, "I don't know what got into me." Or even, "The devil made me do it." Because our conscious mind has not acknowledged these hidden traits, they are apt to express themselves in disguised or distorted ways, in impulsive actions we don't understand.

## Shadow Hurt

Because our unacknowledged Shadow is there as a bottled-up energy, it can suddenly impel us to hurtful and destructive actions that in a more controlled moment we wouldn't want to do. Journalist Seymour Hersh reported one such incident during the Vietnam War.

> A member of Capt. Ernest Medina's company said some men in the unit had turned into "wild animals" two days before the alleged My Lai massacre in Vietnam, beating children and stomping a friendly peasant woman to death. "Why in God's name does this have to happen?" Sgt. Gregory Olsen, 20, asked in a letter to his father. "These are all seemingly normal guys; some were friends of mine. For a while they were like wild animals."[5]

Those young soldiers had tried to repress their fear of death and their hatred of those they held to be responsible for the danger they were in. When suddenly presented with their "enemies," they erupted in a fury of barbaric behavior that appalled their comrades. Their beating young children and brutally kicking helpless women to death became a prelude to the My Lai massacre perpetrated by that same military unit shortly afterwards.

The driver who plowed into the funeral procession in Belfast may have snapped under the frustration of trying to control people who didn't want him in their city. And the mourners who pulled him and his companion from the car and beat them in a burst of rage acted out of years of repressed grief, fear, and resentment.

Similar incidents abound. The fear and hatred deep in his personal Shadow help explain the conduct of an Israeli soldier in the Occupied Territories when he came across two masked Palestinian boys writing slogans on a wall. At point-blank range he shot and killed the boys. Then, as though to crush his own inner demons of anxiety and insecurity, he stomped on the boys' heads. The ferocity of his reaction shocked onlookers.[6]

The Shadow helps explain the behavior of the high-ranking military officer in the second quote at the beginning of the chapter. He had suppressed his feelings of guilt and anxiety, as he had to do in order to keep analyzing nuclear weapons in the abstract coldness of facts and figures. But when the speaker caused him to face the human misery that would result from his nuclear tactics, the unfaced forces in his Shadow broke out in wrath at her.

## Enemy Thinking

Another unfortunate effect of our Shadow is that it makes us unusually alert to those very flaws in others that we refuse to face in ourselves. If laziness is in my Shadow, I can spot it easily in someone else who is taking a break from work. If deep down I want to control others, I quickly feel—and resent—efforts on the part of others to control me. Sometimes our Shadow encourages us to project these distasteful characteristics on people who don't actually have them. But we think they do, with the same unpleasant result. We dislike them because we imagine they are lazy, self-righteous, or greedy. When we find, or imagine, our Shadow traits in others, we tend to dislike them precisely because we dislike those characteristics in ourselves.

Our reaction may be stronger than dislike. It may emerge as contempt and antagonism. Jung would say our hostility is our unconscious way of trying to destroy these tendencies that really lodge deep inside of ourselves. We strive to create a degree of equilibrium within by punishing others for the traits we would really like to remove from ourselves. When our Shadow propels us into hostile actions toward others, it's a hostility of our own making because we're reacting to something in ourselves we anxiously don't want to face. By feeling antagonistic toward someone who is greedy or lazy—or whom we imagine to be—we are seeking to counter our own gnawing but unfaced greed or laziness, in order to relieve our internal anxiety.

Writer Sam Keen has pointed out that we can get a good clue to the context of our own Shadow by looking at the array of people we don't like, and focusing on exactly what it is in them that irritates us.

> Depth psychology has presented us with the undeniable wisdom that the enemy is constructed from denied aspects of the self. Therefore, the radical commandment "Love your enemy as yourself" points the way toward both self-knowledge and peace. We do, in fact, love or hate our enemies to the same degree that we love or hate ourselves. In the image of the enemy, we will find the mirror in which we may see our own face most clearly.[7]

More than likely, we'll find in our enemies the very characteristics in our own makeup that we have covered over or masked from view. What we don't face in ourselves, we're going to be upset with in others.

## Social Poison

This pattern of focusing on a real or imagined flaw in certain people and disliking them because of it contributes to the poisoning of society. When our Shadow helps us dislike people we consider lazy, and when they also happen to be economically poor, it's easy to lapse into blaming the victim. "They're poor because they're lazy. It's their own fault. They should get out and get a job and work for a living." We feel relieved of whatever responsibility we might have for their plight—our complicity in the shutdown of jobs in the area when a business moves to Mexico; or our support of an attack on Iraq instead of supporting a campaign for decent housing.

Good people don't like to admit being racially prejudiced. Racism is not socially acceptable. But we can quickly spot racism in others, to whom we can then feel morally superior. Many "good" people avoid socializing across color lines, and are alert to take protective measures when "they" are around. After all, one has to be prudent. There's no sense in taking a chance. As *The Economist* reported:

> Walled cities, popular in medieval Italy, are making a comeback in suburban America. Leisure World stands on the edge of Laguna Hills in Southern California, where new malls and motorways have been carved out of parched land. Guards at its gates check the identities of those who come and go. Cinder-block walls topped by barbed wire surround it. It is patrolled night and day.[8]

Most of the residents of Leisure World would not admit that racism had anything to do with their decision to move there. It's just that one can't be too safe in Southern California these days, not with the gang wars and riots and ethnic antagonisms. Better safe than sorry. Let's find a place away from "them," move in with our own kind, and make sure that the guards at the gates are well-armed. The result is continued deterioration of city centers, and continued danger from desperate people living violently in a poisoned social climate.

## Ultimate Weakness

One of the most common characteristics found in Shadows is a sense of inadequacy, of weakness, of vulnerability. Everyone experiences some degree of personal insecurity in the face of life's challenges. But on a deeper level our sense of vulnerability stems from realizing the precariousness of our existence. We know we're going to die. At some point in the future, distant or near, we will cease to be as we are now. Our life as we know it will stop. The

threat of termination can be terrifying. Most people simply refuse to think about it. Our inevitable death is shoved into the
depths of our Shadow. It is the most vicious of the Furies that
harass us, the one we're most anxious to ignore into oblivion.

A common way of accommodating this Fury, of compensa-
ting for the terror of termination, is to seek to control as much
of our immediate surroundings as we can. We may not recognize
what is behind our drive for power, but a repressed fear of death
could well be emerging when we seem desperate to influence
people and events around us. Few escape such a drive. We are
easily drawn into the illusion that power over others is a way to
compensate for our feelings of vulnerability. We seek it, and we
often get it. But power achieved doesn't provide the relief it
promised. Just the opposite, in fact. Psychologist Israel Charny
described how the drive for power turns out to be a trap.

> No matter how much people may strut and boast
> about their new majesty, they cannot help but be
> aware that they still have not become masters of their
> destiny and that they will never be free of the ul-
> timate terrors of life and death. They may then be-
> come increasingly desperate and increasingly angry at
> how life still cruelly mocks them. Now their newly
> gained power is no longer cause for celebration but
> demands more and more bolstering. Power now be-
> gets more power-seeking.[9]

When a person is caught in this trap, anxiety increases. We
become susceptible to other ways that promise to assuage it.

## Collective Infections

We may be relatively calm when we're by ourselves, but in
the company of others who begin doing dark, primitive things,
we are tempted to join in. The repressed anger and bitterness in
our Shadow impels us into what psychoanalyst M.L. von Franz

called "collective infections." Bill Buford in his insider study of mob violence, *Among the Thugs*, described a frightening scene he witnessed in England when fans of a losing soccer team suddenly became a frenzied force. They rampaged through the streets shouting obscenities, breaking windows, and beating up innocent bystanders who happened to be in their way. We're becoming uncomfortably accustomed to similar sights in this country, following not a loss but a victory—when a team wins the World Series, the Super Bowl, or the NBA playoffs. All too often the celebration in the winning city turns ugly. Because collective infections have drawn many ordinary people beyond property destruction and into the quicksand of killing, we need to be alert to their intensifying pressure. They were frequently evident during the atrocities of the Nazi Holocaust, feeding on the lethal forces lurking in the Shadow of otherwise respectable people. Most of the Holocaust atrocities were perpetrated not by sadistic killers, but by men and women who, before the Nazi fever, were "good" people leading ordinary lives.

Such was a group of middle-aged Germans from Hamburg, the subject of a recent study by Christopher Browning. Before the war they had been longshoremen and truck drivers, construction workers and machine operators. Some were salesmen, others had office jobs. All were too old for combat. They had grown up in the years before the Nazis came to power, and had known other politics and other moral standards. They seemed an unlikely group to become involved in mass murder. Drafted into a separate police unit, they were given rudimentary military training, then shipped to occupied Poland. They were assigned to a "special task," the nature of which they were not informed in advance. When they arrived in Poland, they learned that their mission was to be the cold-blooded killing of Jews. Some were shocked and horrified. A few refused and were given other assignments. But most of them went along with the unit.

One of the men later recalled their preparation for the "special task."

> Our battalion physician...had to explain to us pre-
> cisely how we had to shoot in order to induce the im-
> mediate death of the victim. I remember exactly that
> for this demonstration he drew or outlined the con-
> tour of a human body, at least from the shoulders up-
> ward, and then indicated precisely the point on
> which the fixed bayonet was to be placed as an aim-
> ing guide...at the neck.[10]

On their first mission some of the men rounded up the villagers and marched them off into the nearby woods. Others were
detached to form the shooting detail. The results that first time
were gruesome.

> Through the point-blank shot that was thus required,
> the bullet struck the head of the victim at such a tra-
> jectory that often the entire skull or at least the en-
> tire rear skullcap was torn off, and blood, bone
> splinters, and brains sprayed everywhere and be-
> smirched the shooters.[11]

At the end of their first massacre, most of the men were de-
pressed, angry, and shaken. They couldn't eat. Their officers provided generous quantities of alcohol and many got quite drunk.

After several similar missions, most of them became hardened to the unpleasant task and hunkered down to fulfill what
they were told was their duty, ordered by "higher authorities."
Many later said that an important element in their acquiescence
was the desire not to appear weak in the eyes of their comrades.
Those who refused the assignment were looked upon as cow-
ardly. Besides the overt authoritarian atmosphere and the peer
pressure to conform, dark forces from their Shadow were at
work. Almost all harbored negative racial stereotypes of Jews.
Newly added to their Shadow was the frustration of being torn
from their ordinary lives. They had to cope, too, with the brutal-

ization that always results when men are armed and sent to kill one another on the massive scale of a war. The violence these men perpetrated provides a sobering image of the extremes to which "good" people can be pushed by powerful forces at work around—and in—them.

## Knowing the Shadow

Because the Shadow has played a significant role in many massacres over the millennia, we need to be sensitive to what Jung called "its nefarious doings" if we would avert future massacres over the horizon. Exploring my own Shadow not only helps me become a more balanced, wholesome person, but it also keeps me from creating misery for others. As an old Zen Buddhist Master said, we must follow the example of the cowherd "who watches his ox with a stick so that it will not graze on other people's meadows."

Keeping a constant eye on our Shadow ox can harness its energy and turn it to positive good. What we're after is getting to know our Shadow, not necessarily eliminating its contents. Our more effective wholeness comes from self-realization, knowing what's inside of us, accepting ourselves, tapping our deepest energies. When we do that, we abandon our illusion of perfection. We face what we really are, warts and all. And we have a lot more there in our depths than warts. In Charny's words:

> deep within our human experiencing, there is, along with our potential destructiveness, a reverence for life...[which] must at least be equal to the power [of] destroying life.[12]

When we take the plunge, when we stir around in the darkness of our psyche to see what's really there, we can shine the light of hope on it—the hope that we can come to grips with it. We can look the Shadow in the eye, and make it a friend. While this self-facing will not, can not, should not do away with the energies that make up our unique self, it will help us to harness these energies into more wholesome directions—at least more often than we would if we left them to their own devices.

This rich mixture of negative and positive forces deep within us frequently surfaces in expressions of our sexuality. It is to that sensitive area of our conscious and unconscious self that we next turn in our efforts to grasp more fully why good people do bad things.

*There seems to be such a thing as sex, defined as a union of bodies. Foreplay. Coitus—intercourse. In reality, there is no such thing. There is only a union of persons.*

—Gerard Sloyan

# CHAPTER FIVE

# THE S-WORD

"A scathing pentagon report accused more than 140 naval officers of misconduct in the infamous 1991 Tailhook convention. In graphic terms, the report outlines a three-day bacchanal where men and women engaged in public sex, nudity and excessive drinking, and dozens of women were pushed through a 'gauntlet' of groping, pawing pilots. The report said 23 officers were found to have participated in sexual assaults and an additional 23 in indecent exposure."[1]

"His name is Reginald. He's 27, served in the 101st Army Airborne, and he brags about the muscles on the arms of his 10 year-old son. When we met, I was

on my way home with a supermarket salad and he was
in the dive position atop a railing on the bridge over
the Wolf River. 'Wait!' I screamed from the driver's
seat. 'What are you doing? Please don't, please don't,'
I begged. He turned around and looked at me. Then,
in a tone of frustration, he said, 'I'm just tired of it all.
I'm gay and I'm tired of getting beat up.' He talked
about having been shot here in Memphis. Finally, he
agreed to come down. The instant he hit the sidewalk, a cadre of police officers tackled and handcuffed
him."[2]

MOST "GOOD" PEOPLE want to be considered normal.
But so much confusion abounds these days about what is normal
in sexuality that many avoid talking about it, or restrict it to
conversations with a very few people with whom they are most
comfortable. Society's attitude toward sexuality is ambivalent.
On the one hand we see widespread acceptance of unmarried
couples living together, and of "adult" entertainment in bars and
restaurants. Sexuality is exploited in advertising, and increasing
sexual explicitness appears in television, movies, and magazines.
Many openly proclaim what used to be considered deviant sexual preferences. But we also have forceful voices criticizing all of
this, and not just conservative newspaper columnists and fundamentalist religious preachers. Many concerned observers feel
that the sexual revolution, although valuable in breaking down
taboos and opening up new richness in human relationships, has
gone too far. They suspect that something fundamental is being
undermined. Overshadowing everything sexual is the specter of
AIDS.

Sometimes a source gives out mixed messages. The same
newspaper that editorializes against the availability of por-
nography accepts ads for topless clubs. A preacher who rails
against homosexuality is found in the company of a prostitute.
Schools advocate abstinence, but also teach safe sex and some

distribute condoms. Good people want to be sensitive to the voices of women who point out the inequalities they have suffered from male dominant social structures. But when the voices seem too shrill, it's not easy to sift out their truth.

Clergy of our religious institutions are divided. Some priests, ministers, and rabbis preach that sex outside marriage is a sin. Others are lenient and tolerant. Because of the lack of religious consensus, Paul Brown, a Presbyterian minister and seminary professor, observed, "The 'S-word' is rarely mentioned in worship." He suggested two reasons for the absence of sexual concerns in liturgical language. One reason is that

> historically the church has been ambiguous about how it regards sex—as sinful, dangerous, a biological necessity, or as altogether personal and therefore private. Another reason may be that current sexual practices and attitudes are so fluid and pluralistic, even among Christians, that the church can say very little about human sexuality that is definitive or unequivocal.[3]

Even though the sexual dimension is seldom mentioned in worship and does not often turn up in polite conversations, it is inevitably present in our personal lives and social interactions. It has deep roots in our innermost being, roots that are often not faced and lurk in our Shadow ready to emerge unexpectedly, especially under the pressure of a collective infection. Charny described an incident where some otherwise "good" young people found themselves swept along into a confusion of sexual exploitation.

> It was an innocent starlit night in the oar house of a summer camp. We were counselors to the campers by day and busy with our burgeoning teenage sexuality by night. It started teasingly, deliciously enough, with

a dare that evening that any female counselor caught walking past a certain grove of trees would be subjected to the fullest measure of the law of the male counselors. Several girls accepted the obvious invitation, and to everyone's great delight were taken to the oar house amid peals of laughter mixed with mock protests.

However, once in the oar house, a strange process began to build. There soon arose from among us a leader to direct the unfolding drama....With consummate concentration, he led the ceremony, and truth be told, the rest of us cowards and cheap thrill seekers piggybacked on the leader's taking charge.

Before long, we had become Enjoyers of the Spectacle of our Leader commanding the Disrobing of the Lasses. The rule was that those girls who acknowledged the error of their ways in walking onto the male "campus" were to be set free but those who refused to throw themselves on the mercy of the court were to be subjected to disrobing. For awhile longer, there was still laughter, though now it was increasingly nervous and tension-charged. Before long, the simple scene turned before our very eyes into a stark drama of stubborn pride, then increasing hurt, and finally even panic.

As the Leader continued resolutely in his methodical Prosecution of Justice, an increasingly ugly, sadistic beat began to pulsate in the Disrobing. More and more, the girls pleaded to be set loose, and a frenzy of hysteria and panic began to mount. Fortunately, the camp director arrived on the scene, and the episode was brought to an end, but not before all of us experienced a profound sense of shock that we had turned into groups of Oppressors and Victims.[4]

Because of sexuality's deep roots and uncertain expression, it's no wonder that the church is ambiguous and society is ambivalent. As we gingerly seek the right approach to sexuality, we can see in a new light patterns of thought and behavior displayed by many "good" people that continue to cause damage.

## Homophobia

Discrimination against homosexual people has long been with us. In recent years it's been muted by the increase in understanding and sensitivity toward people's sexual orientation. But it's still all too often part of the atmosphere where we work, or built into the practices of the school or church to which we belong. And people are hurt by it.

In the early 1970s a former student of mine, a bright, handsome young man, invited Janice and me to look him up if we were ever in the South Florida area, where he lived with his parents. On a spring break trip a few months later we did call him, and received an invitation to meet him at a party. When we found the address we entered a room full of men in animated conversations, pleasant, welcoming. In the course of the evening he took us aside and said he wanted us to know he was gay. He had invited us to the party to introduce us to some of his friends. He really couldn't tell his parents, he said. He was feeling considerable pressure from leading a hidden life, but he feared the disgrace he would face if he came out of the closet. Less than a year later he committed suicide. We were shocked to hear about it. But his party, and the people we met there, launched Janice and me into an investigation and a new understanding of homosexuality.

The emotional and spiritual wounds suffered when homosexual men and women are marginalized or rejected can be more damaging than bodily wounds inflicted by physical violence. The man named Reginald, in the second news story at the beginning of this chapter, expressed the pain he had felt for years that led him to the bridge. Perhaps, after being rescued, he would find relief. But perhaps not. The discrimination that plagued Reginald, and that drove my former student to suicide, is still very much alive in our society.

We now know that the root of much homophobia is insecurity about one's own sexuality. This insecurity leads to seeking reassurance through denigrating people whose sexual orientation is different from one's own. Putting others down, pointing out what is considered their sexual failure, can make one feel less poorly about one's own inadequacy.

Men seem more prone to this pattern than women. Because most cultures until recently have assumed that men are dominant, are superior, ought to be in charge, men have been pressured to emphasize what have been trumpeted as masculine traits: toughness, effectiveness. Conversely, we were taught to repress what were considered feminine traits, such as tenderness and emotional expressiveness. Men usually assumed that their sexual expression ought to emphasize the toughness and effectiveness they thought were expected of them in society. When in their heart of hearts they were not sure they could live up to this model in their sexual performance, they tended to overemphasize these characteristics in their overall behavior. At the same time, they denigrated men who displayed prototypical feminine traits. It happens, though, that most gay men do not display prototypical feminine traits. Most are indistinguishable in their appearance and manner from straight men, who themselves display a wide range of differences. The presumption of femininity was challenged by men in military service who revealed their homosexual orientation. As writer Richard Rodriguez observed, "It was easy for Americans to tolerate homosexuals as long as homosexuals were sissies. It is another matter altogether for many American heterosexuals to accept the idea of sissy warriors."[5]

Uncertainty about their ability to dominate sexually is the root of the irrational fear of homosexuality found in many men. Having sexual feelings toward another man is thought to be a sign of unmanliness, of failed masculinity. It is felt to imply be-

ing dominated rather than dominating, and is profoundly un-
settling. It threatens to throw out of kilter the whole pattern of a
man's life, to turn upside down the fundamental thrust of his in-
terpersonal relations based on being in charge. Homosexuality is
called, often with intense feeling, "queer," or "perverted."

Bruce Kokopeli and George Lakey showed how the desire
to express one's masculinity by controlling another person could
produce homosexual acts that were not at all the result of homosexual orientation.

> In prisons, for example, men can be respected if they
> fuck other men, but not if they are themselves fucked.
> (We used the word "fucked" intentionally for its am-
> biguity.) Often prison rapes are done by men who
> identify as heterosexual; one hole substitutes for an-
> other in this scene, for sex is in either case an expres-
> sion of domination for the masculine mystique.[6]

A dictionary gives two meanings for the word "fuck." One is to
have sexual intercourse; the other is to treat someone unfairly or
harshly. At times the two meanings are intensely intertwined in
a particular behavior episode. When a man seeks to express his
mistaken notion of masculinity through his domination of a
woman, the act of sexual intercourse is engaged in less with tenderness and mutuality, and more with force and pain.

Not only the double-meaning act to which it refers, but
the word itself has been considered a male preserve. Many wom-
en have only recently begun to use it in public. Pediatrician and
peace activist Helen Caldicott related what happened to her on
one occasion when she used the word to emphasize her strong
feelings. She had been invited to speak on a television program
with a retired brigadier general.

> For ten minutes he talked in a calm, polite way about
> nuclear war and the possibility of the world being

blown up....As the arc lights were turned off at the end, he turned to me and aggressively said, "You should go to Russia." I thought for several seconds, decided to let him see the true fear in my soul, and said to him, "I fucking want my kids to grow up." Well, he could talk with absolutely no emotion about nuclear war and the deaths of hundreds of millions of human beings, but when a lady said "fuck" to him, he was undone. He went wild and almost physically attacked me. The producer came running out to separate us; there was nearly a brawl on the floor of the TV studio.[7]

## Military Sexism

Sexual insecurity and confusion, leading to the kind of abusive, immature behavior exhibited in the Tailhook scandal referred to at the beginning of the chapter, are commonplace among men in military service. Once one considers the mission of the military and the training that leads to fitness for that mission, such behavior is not surprising. The primary purpose of the military is to force another group of people, labeled "the enemy," to submit to "our" will. Military force is the ultimate exercise in domination, requiring the inflicting of death if other means of intimidation fail. Military training is orchestrated to ensure not only the ability, but above all the willingness, to create this kind of pressure. To do that, military people have to be "tough."

In basic training, young men still unsure of their individual identities are forced to adopt exaggerated expressions of masculine strength. Signs of weakness are squelched. Since weakness is considered to be "feminine," they are taught to hate the feminine in themselves, and are offered a distorted masculinity based on aggression and dominance. One consequence is the readiness of all too many military men to engage in gay bashing. Paradoxically, at the same time men in military service are taught to be tough, they are also required to be "feminine" in the sense of themselves being dominated by their superiors in the chain of command. They are systematically taught to obey orders instantly and without question. Writer and professor Cynthia Adcock described this pressure as a double bind:

> [Military] men must be both submissive and dominating. To live in a double bind situation creates a terrible need to be aggressive, assertive, violent toward someone else. That someone becomes an "Other," a female or a male enemy.[8]

The requirement of complete and instant submission to authority is similar to child abuse in that it creates the desire to abuse and dominate others in turn. Sexual abuse in the form of rape is so common in time of war that it's a taken-for-granted by-product of combat.

The ultimate reinforcement of military masculinity lies in the myth that combat is ennobling. "Myth" here is used in two senses. One meaning is a powerful idea that grips the imagination. "Combat" conveys the image of a heroic endeavor. The ordeal of engaging in direct physical struggle with an enemy is the supreme test of a real man. It is the opportunity to prove one's manhood in direct confrontation with another who would impose his will on me unless I prove to be the stronger. The one who emerges victorious truly deserves the prestigious title of "warrior." This is the image of combat that permeates military lore.

The other meaning of "myth" is a false interpretation of reality. The image of noble combat masks the central reality of what war is really like. Actual combat is a dirty, fear-filled ugliness of one's own threatened extinction, coupled with the hobbling guilt that comes from terminating other human lives. The reality of military service, which prepares for combat, involves subservience, obedience, and almost total dependence on superiors and on the other people in one's unit. But because the full reality is seldom faced before a war, "combat"—in the abstract— is seen as a shining opportunity for self-realization.

And, of course, for those who accept the myth in the first sense, "combat" simply cannot involve women. If women, embodying the dreaded weakness, were seen as able to engage in combat, the carefully nurtured structure of male aggressiveness necessary to subdue an enemy by lethal force would be undermined. A common-sense glance at the technology of modern warfare shows that women can fly the planes, launch the missiles, and steer the ships every bit as skillfully as men. Military leaders sometimes seem to be grasping at straws when they try to give rational explanations why women should not be permitted in combat in the face of such obvious awareness. One such effort by a former Marine Commandant, though, gave away the hidden secret.

> War is man's work. Biological convergence on the battlefield would not only be dissatisfying in terms of what women could do, but it would be an enormous psychological distraction for the male who wants to think that he's fighting for that woman somewhere behind, not up there in the same foxhole with him. It tramples the male ego. When you get right down to it, you've got to protect the manliness of war.[9]

The "manliness of war" carries with it the unfortunate consequence of despising feminine characteristics in men, and masculine characteristics in women. It underlies the stringent efforts to expel homosexual men and women from military service, and helps explain the strong opposition from top military leaders when President Bill Clinton said he was going to lift that ban. It's not that homosexual people are physically unfit for the duties demanded of them. It's that their presence has a psychologically upsetting effect on a military organization fundamentally premised on masculine domination.

This "manliness of war" also leads to the regrettable sexual exploitation of women in the prostitution industry that invariably springs up around military installations. Because the key dynamic of military manliness is domination, it is no surprise that such exploitation often involves cruelty and callousness; it is sometimes sadistic sexuality, frequently with racist overtones. As Janice and I recognized in Olongapo City next to what was then the Subic Bay Naval Base in the Philippines, most of the relatively large-statured sailors and marines, whether Caucasian or African-American, had contempt for what they saw as the Little Brown Filipinas they used and abused. Cynthia Eloe outlined the consistency between military masculinity, racism, and sexism:

> The women who work in bars, brothels, and massage parlors around military bases are frequently non-white and non-European, unlike most of the male soldiers they are expected to attract. This situation reinforces the global dynamics of sexism and racism that have played an important historical role in colonialization and military expansion. In the microcosm of the base, soldier-clients learn to view their masculinity—and the prowess of the nation they represent—as dependent on their sexual domination of the women who live near the base.[10]

Most "good" people outside the military can understand the dynamic of domination at work in military masculinity. But because it's so inextricably tied in with the whole ethos of the military system which is linked to the nation's defense, the underlying sexual issues are hardly ever addressed. Gay bashing, sexual racism, and exploitation around military bases are shrugged off as necessary, although unpleasant, facts of life.

## Harassment Uncertainty

Because of blundering due to our socialization and our culture, "good" people often do things that are offensive to the opposite sex. It may be obvious, such as a gender-discriminatory salary scale, or a bias in promotion policy—the "glass ceiling" barrier. It may be more subtle, an unconscious, indeliberate hurt inflicted by word or deed. It may be a misunderstanding or misinterpretation of an innocent remark. We are now much more aware that people suffer from practices formerly considered acceptable or normal. Most "good" people would like to recognize these practices and avoid being responsible for them. Once alerted, it's easy to spot blatant sex discrimination. But the subtle possibilities of harassment inherent in heterosexual interaction need more careful attention. Where men and women are together, the possibility of misunderstanding always exists. William Broyles, Jr., former editor-in-chief of *Newsweek*, observed:

> I have seen highly professional, otherwise respectable men commit sexual harassment, just as I have seen highly professional, otherwise capable women imagine relationships that did not exist...and contrive harassment charges to revenge other slights or to advance themselves.[11]

Some sexual tension is going to be present in any male-female relationship. It's one of the things that makes an opposite-sex friendship interesting and rewarding. It also makes an opposite-sex friendship delicate and tricky. Because of social conditioning, men often feel that they should initiate the communication. In doing so, they open themselves up to the possibility of embarrassment and misunderstanding. Women want to be treated equally, but most also want to be considered attractive. What is attractive and pleasing to the sight for one man may be felt to be provocative and giving come-on signals by another. The possibility for misjudging—on both sides—is considerable. Opposite-sex friendship is also tricky because a platonic relationship can evolve into a sexual one. It can happen on the part of both people, or on the part of just one. Navigating successfully in heterosexual interactions takes considerable skill and sensitivity. Most of us hope we can tune in sufficiently to avoid bumbling around and upsetting others, while appreciating the richness heterosexual association offers.

## Learning to Listen

I was brought up in a family with two other males: my father and brother, and three females: my mother and two sisters. In our pre-adolescent years we children were much more aware of growing up together in our home, our neighborhood, and our schools, and not very aware that our gender differences were significant. Our parents did what parents were supposed to do: make a living and make a home.

In high school I discovered girls. And "girls" weren't like my sisters. "Girls" were exotic creatures, interesting, and attractive. I went to dances and had "crushes," but never really got to know them very well. My all-boys high school and my all-male college left me pretty much in the dark. I took for granted the widespread assumption of those times that men ran the world, women stayed home, and "girls" could supply sexual adventure. When I studied philosophy and read that Aristotle and Aquinas considered women to be "misbegotten males," conceived when an unfortunate south wind was blowing,[12] I didn't think it was a very scientific analysis, but I didn't really get upset about it either. At that time I took for granted that women were the weaker sex, that they were subject to unpredictable temperaments, and that one had to be wary of their wiles.

I count as one of my greatest blessings the opportunity to teach at an all-women's college in the early 1960s. There I discovered that women in the classroom were just as bright as men and sometimes brighter. I also learned that women were every bit as competent and conscientious as teachers and administrators. The women I got to know there were indeed very much like my mother and sisters in responding positively to a straightforward approach in any personal or professional interactions. I also discovered that instead of being mysterious and manipulative and difficult, they were really very nice to be with. I liked them.

Besides learning how to be more at ease in my associations, I made an important intellectual discovery at that college. My attention was called to the dawning women's equality movement. Simone de Beauvoir's *The Second Sex* was just making its appearance. A few students and colleagues, gently and sensitively I later came to appreciate, pointed out the incorrectness of a male-dominant culture and, by implication, my male-superiority assumptions. When Janice and I married at the end of the 1960s we tried to approach each other with a sense of equality and respect. Over the decades we have found ourselves growing in mutual appreciation. We haven't solved the sexual inequality arrangements we sometimes find ourselves in at home, or the sexual harassment problems we sometimes encounter at work. But we are more aware of them and less likely to be caught by surprise.

In the movie *White Men Can't Jump*, the African-American basketball player, responding to his white partner's marital problems, laid out an axiom: "Always listen to the woman." His friend replied plaintively," "But I listened to you, instead!" His retort: "That was your mistake. If you would have listened to her and not me, you wouldn't be in the mess you're in now." I've found his axiom, "Always listen to the woman," to be very good advice for men. We may not always agree with what we hear, but I've been spared many mistakes and received much valuable advice through such listening.

As we seek to probe further into the thicket of thoughts and feelings of those "good" people who sometimes do bad things, we need to look at another S-word that figures prominently: the religious experience of Salvation.

*We are all caught in an inescapable network of mutuality, tied into a single garment of destiny.*
—Martin Luther King, Jr.

CHAPTER SIX

# PERSONAL SALVATION

"On a dusty side street near the Mississippi River levee, a former carnival operator who never finished high school built a lucrative business fueled by used, dirty motor oil. While the oil operations made William Gurley a wealthy man, they also left Crittenden County with two of the nation's worst hazardous-waste sites. Pits where Gurley's refining sludge was dumped contain toxic metals, long-lasting chlorinated compounds and cancer-causing petrochemicals—wastes that are expected to cost well over $10 million to clean up. So far, however, the government has been unable to collect any money for cleanup from Gurley. 'I've just been flabbergasted. This guy is truly avoiding his responsibilities,' said David Weeks of the U.S. Environmental Protection Agency. Gurley also is deeply religious. 'He's probably as honest an individual as you'll find,' said a friend who attended church with Gurley."[1]

"The Reverend Charles Jones was at his most ebullient when talking about the impending end times: 'Brother, we've not seen hard times like there shall be when God comes to settle the score here on this earth. God's going to do something to this earth. Man, I'm not going to be here. I'm going to be in glory with Jesus 'cause I've been saved.'"[2]

AT THE HEART OF ALL RELIGION is an experience of salvation. It's a feeling that one's life is significantly improved by entering into harmony with the ultimate pattern of the universe. In all religions the final stage of salvation is believed to occur beyond the flow of ordinary life, whether in merging with Absolute Reality, or as eternal life in the glorified condition of Heaven or Paradise. This ultimate, complete fulfillment is a goal fervently desired by a religion's faithful followers. It brings relief from the undesirable conditions of suffering, frailty, finitude, and sin that stain one's present life. It will be a total release from the world's woes, and absolute security from all threatening forces.

Salvation begins while a person is still struggling with this present life. It increases as one continues along the way prescribed by the religion in the confidence that this way is the right one for *me*. For a Hindu, the way might be faithful fulfillment of daily duties in the awareness of an unseen Power, hoping for liberation from the cycle of death and rebirth. For a Buddhist, salvation is found in faithfully following the noble truths that overcome radical selfishness and lead to *Nirvana*. The three great monotheistic religions of the West proclaim a single all-powerful God who created the world. Salvation starts when people begin shaping their lives according to God's plan. These three religions profess that God has communicated the right course of action to guide one in the midst of a muddled world—through the Torah in Judaism, Jesus the Son of God in Christianity, and the Koran in Islam.

With the feeling of having entered into the way of salvation, life's gloom becomes suffused with a measure of joy. Although the gloom is never entirely dissipated because of the persistence of evil, and of tragic flaws like disease, death, and natural disasters, a believer finds joy in the hope that all these will eventually be overcome. In the meantime, he or she finds consolation in being on the path to ultimate victory, like the minister quoted at the beginning of the chapter. He was confident that, despite hard times ahead, he would be all right because he's been saved.

"Jesus saves" is the cornerstone belief of Christianity. Those who were raised in a Christian family experienced a way of coping with our youthful failures, and a strong confidence that, no matter what, God was in control of our world—and we were in touch with God. Writer Gerard Straub described a salvation experience coming later in life to a woman who had not felt it earlier. It happened at home, while she was watching a television evangelist.

> Her eyes dance with emotion, while meditatively gazing at the flickering images. Her attention is held captive by a preacher. She is exhorted to join him in prayer, confess her sinfulness, and invite Jesus into her heart. The camera lens studies the preacher's tightly closed eyes and forehead frown. The woman is entranced by the intensity of his prayer. "Lord Jesus, I am a sinner," she cries, having engaged his reality. She prays that Jesus will bestow his mercy upon her. The prayer ends with the timeless sound that comprises the word Amen. She is born again.[3]

A taste of salvation like this is a valuable, life-enhancing experience. One's doubt and confusion, one's inadequacy in the face of the problems that plague each day are counteracted by feeling that one is in harmony with a Higher Power, a Savior. It provides an antidote to the lurking fear of chaos and evil. It fosters a hope of liberation from all oppression. And it gives a sense of meaning to what seems like the randomness and darkness of the day.

Because human life inevitably involves interaction with people, any experience of salvation includes some way of understanding how best to live with others. Considering only Christianity, we see a wide variety of emphases. Although Jesus did say that the Great Commandment has two dimensions: a vertical one—love God above all things, and a horizontal one—love one's neighbor as oneself; interpretations about what these mean in practice have varied widely in its more than 20,000 denominations. Each group or subgroup provides its own setting and its own slant on salvation; each is influenced by the cultural context of its traditions and the immediate surroundings of its present expression. All Christians have some attitude toward the world around them and the society in which they live. We can identify two broad approaches: those who believe it's important to enter the affairs of the world to improve conditions, and those who don't.

## Social Responsibility

Many Christians have believed that love of neighbor means taking up responsibility for counteracting social ills. They would work vigorously to change the world in the direction they believe is for the better. In the 19th century, Christians in the United States were in the forefront of the movement to abolish slavery. Toward the end of the century, many became involved in what was known as the Social Gospel, which developed in the wake of the Industrial Revolution. With the concentration of economic power into fewer hands, seriously unequal distribution of wealth, and the growth of vast cities with their slums, many Christians tried to ameliorate these conditions.

They favored the rights of workers to organize, pressed for the end of child labor, advocated a minimum wage, and sought to reduce poverty, especially in the degrading living conditions of large cities. Historian Sydney Ahlstrom called the Social Gospel movement "the most distinctive contribution of the American churches to world Christianity."[4]

In the 20th century, many Catholics were inspired by the Second Vatican Council's reminder: "It has pleased God to make people holy and save them not merely as individuals without any mutual bonds, but by making them into a single people, a people which acknowledges Him in truth and serves Him in holiness."[5] Martin Luther King had expressed that same sense of mutuality in the context of the Civil Rights Movement: "Whatever affects one directly affects all indirectly. For some strange reason I can never be what I ought to be until you are what you ought to be. And you can never be what you ought to be until I am what I ought to be. This is the way God's universe is made; this is the way it is structured."[6] This intense feeling of relatedness, coupled with the conviction that the law of love demands improving social structures, led to an outburst of energy in the decades that followed.

Theologian Edward Schillebeeckx said that the peace of Christ in our time consists "in an inward discontent, in a prophetic protest against the situation as it is, and which is precisely not right the way it is."[7] The situation of the world is not right because far too many people lack access to the basic necessities of food, clothing, shelter, medical care, and employment. The prophetic protest against the situation includes a judicious mix of religious inspiration and social action.

## Individualism

But this prophetic protest has not been expressed by a majority of Christians. A common theme in the United States has always been an emphasis on the individual. "Rugged individualism," extolled in the American myth, permeates much of our culture, including our religion. One can see it at work when believers experience salvation and remain indifferent or powerless in the face of social problems. One instance would be a typical country congregation in Mississippi. On any given Sunday at church the congregation will be all black or all white. For six days a week, black or white, they will be struggling to scratch out a living in a resistant environment. The Sunday experience of the Bible's permanence and the preacher's certainties brings some relief from the daily grind. After church they will go back, good people all, to a racially suspicious climate. Most will be content not to struggle too hard against ancient prejudices.

In a completely different cultural setting, a typical Irish family in New England has been Catholic for generations. They are comfortable with the conviction that the church, despite its human failings, really does profess the way, the truth, and the life. Whether they go to Mass every Sunday or not, they know that the church, with its salutary sacraments, provides a living link with the Lord. They are busy with their careers and their children's education, and will renew their perennial spring hopes in the Red Sox. They will want whatever party that controls the State House in Boston or the White House in Washington to grant some middle-class tax relief. These good people want good things for themselves, but often and perhaps unconsciously to the exclusion of what is good for others.

The lonely woman who experienced a taste of salvation from the television evangelist will go to work the next day with a new confidence in her step and be more responsive to her coworkers. She will be pleased if she learns that the advertising agency she works for is aggressively expanding its clientele in Latin America. Many of the corporations her agency represents favor the wealthy few, and continue the exploitation of the poor majority who suffer under the unjust structures of their society. But she will probably not reflect on any of this. Her personal life has taken on a new lightness, and for this she is grateful.

The stress on the individual more than on the community, prominent in American culture and American religion, is intensified by the mushrooming communications technology. It has put an end-of-the-century spin on the age-old tendency toward self-absorption. Many of us find ourselves bombarded with images from the television screen, struggling to absorb something from the melange. The very abundance of images has an isolating effect. Everyone who watches television is confronted with his or her own array of stimuli. Social commentator William Greider has described it for us:

> People are now lost in a bewildering display of sound and light, from the random anger of talk radio to the manipulative images of television commercials, from the celebrity culture fostered by mass media to the emotional directness of instant TV news. It is not that people are isolated from public affairs and utterly ignorant....Their problem is that they are inundated with messages—a raging river of information that is fake or true or alluring distraction. As a result, people are reduced to the role of sullen spectators, listening and watching without necessarily believing what they are told.[8]

The same electronics explosion that gives information overload also provides escape—but still in an individualistic mode, as television analyst Joyce Nelson pointed out:

> In the society of the spectacle, the screen is the site of...providing both the illusion of "involvement" and the illusion of "control." As our actual impact on decision-making in the corporate, political, and militarist spheres of society has decreased, the illusion of our "control" has been enhanced through an array of interactive and consumer technologies—television,

video-games, personal computers, microwave ovens—
that seem instantly responsive to our needs, servo-
mechanisms for our desires.[9]

Our personal video screen separates us from others watching their own personal video screens. Our personal computer absorbs us with its fascinating challenge to our creative ingenuity
but in isolation from other human beings. Telecommunications
technology is now experimenting with ways to conduct business
meetings by having individuals in isolated offices type their ideas anonymously on a computer keyboard where the ideas can be
seen and responded to by other participants in the "meeting"
without the interference of human interchange. All these emphases on the individual reinforce the tendency of those who
would refrain from involving themselves in efforts to improve
their society. And so, many devout believers, good people, prefer
to be alone with Jesus, even as members of a Sunday congregation. God knows the secrets of *my* heart. I must repent of *my*
sins. When I die, I will go to heaven by *myself*.

Since those same Christians still have to make a living,
they will engage with the world, but feel uneasy with it. They
may deal with the world on its own terms, take what they can
from it, but try to maintain standards of individual decency in
the process. That's what businessman William Gurley in the
news story at the beginning of this chapter did. He was a regular
churchgoer, known to be honest in his personal dealings, and
opposed to the trappings of what he considered sinful lifestyles.
While setting up operations in the state of Nevada, he refused
even to eat lunch in a casino.

Twenty thousand members of a Memphis fundamentalist
church, one of the largest Christian congregations in the country, voted overwhelmingly to move their church from the decaying central city to a sparkling new complex miles out on the
expressway next to an immaculate, segregated country club.
Most of these good people had faith in their own personal salva-

tion, and little sense of moral responsibility to an urban environment in transition. They felt it wasn't their fault that the city's
infrastructure was deteriorating. Besides, they needed a bigger
building to accommodate all who attended every Sunday in pursuit of personal soothing. It made sense to worship in the comfort their generosity could afford. If the chemical company some
work for exports lethal pesticides to Third World countries,
well, that's too bad, but they're not illegal in those countries,
even if they are banned in the United States. It's very important, though, that the company provides ample medical in-
surance for their family and generous retirement benefits for its
executives. Should these good churchgoers discover that the
military in which their son or daughter serves has a unit that
trains torturers, and another prepared to engage in germ warfare,
they would probably rationalize that it's necessary for the nation's defense. Anyway, that's the Commander-in-Chief's responsibility; it's not their place to question it.

Their individualistic version of religion is widespread, not
only in the United States, but increasingly in the Third World.
Personal-salvation religion can be a soothing antidote to the
pain of poverty. It can also siphon off energy to improve the social environment. In such a climate, forces of greed and exploitation can continue to prosper. In the Philippines, Janice
and I saw what amounted to a surge of Christian fundamentalism, focusing people's spiritual energies on their individual salvation and away from struggling to better their living
conditions. Many Philippine clergy and religious were convinced that this increase of fundamentalism was funded by
American and Korean political conservatives bent on thwarting
the efforts of those Filipinos who would address the social and
economic abuses in their country.

# The Religious Right
Usually coupled with the stress on individualistic salvation
is a concomitant emphasis on individualistic morality. This

means the only sins worth considering are individual sins, usually involving personal dishonesty, misuse of sexuality, or unwarranted violence against others. Many Christians, caught up in this ethos, see much of society as sinful, corrupt, inherently wicked. They hold tenaciously to the answers they themselves have found to life. They are distressed by what they see as society's encroaching immorality: the widespread resort to abortion, the flaunting of suggestive sex, the confusion of gender roles, the tolerance of homosexual lifestyles, and women who seem more devoted to their careers than to their family. Sen. Jesse Helms has given vivid expression to this view:

> ...within my own lifetime, I have seen the most ferocious assaults on Christian faith and morals; first on the part of the intellectual community, and then on the part of the government. Especially in the last 25 years, the federal government has not even tried to conceal its hostility to religion; now, with many of our churches in disarray, the attack is being prepared against the family as the last bastion opposing the totalitarian state. Militant atheists and socialists have gone very far in imposing their view of life and man on almost every American institution.[10]

Many Christians, concerned about these ills, have taken up arms—not literally, yet—to combat these evils. Their prescription is not couched in terms of liberation from oppression, but of restoring a social order of the past. The movement has been labeled the Religious Right. Its agenda includes:

—restoring prayer, meaning Christian prayer, in public schools
—criminalizing abortion
—eliminating sexually explicit material from art and entertainment

—invigorating capital punishment

—minimizing social welfare programs

—strengthening the Armed Forces

—encouraging subsidies for private schools

—keeping women secondary to men, children obedient to parents, and making divorce very difficult

—putting down threats anywhere in the world to America's dominance.[11]

This agenda cuts across denominational lines. Although not identical with fundamentalism, it does include some of its elements. Christian Fundamentalism originated in the early years of the 20th century. It espoused a literal interpretation of the Bible and claimed to draw from the Bible a set of beliefs that were largely characteristic of Victorian society. Other elements in the Religious Right come from what Robert Bellah called America's Civil Religion, the conviction that this nation, a chosen people, was destined by God to lead the world and ensure the prosperity of its own citizens.

## Armageddon Theology

One version of the Religious Right has stressed the imminence of the end of the world and the conviction that true believers will be spared the terrors that precede that end. This belief is rooted in the theological tradition of Pre-millennial Dispensationalism. It was an interpretation of the Scriptures, refined in the 19th century, that saw creation divided into seven "dispensations," or grand epochs of history. Starting with the Age of Innocence in the Garden of Eden, these epochs will culminate in the final fulfillment of time, the Millennium when Christ will come again and rule a peaceful world for a thousand years. The time just before this Millennium will be filled with disasters—waverers abandoning the faith, earthquakes, disturbances in the sky, wars, and civic unrest—climaxing in the battle of Armageddon. After the battle is over, Christ will come

to earth and inaugurate the Millennium. True believers, however, will be spared the worst of the troubles because they will be
snatched up to heaven, "raptured," just before the end.

In recent decades some pre-millennial dispensationalists,
although perhaps not calling themselves by that label, began to
say that nuclear war could very well be God's way of ending the
world by fire, ushering in Armageddon and the Second Coming.
A nuclear holocaust wasn't an unmitigated disaster; it might
well be the fulfillment of the Scriptures. For a while, especially
in the years of Ronald Reagan's first term as president, a number
of influential people expressed this view. Books detailing it,
complete with maps and disaster headlines, sold well. It was a
way of living with the nuclear threat, an alternative to fear and
pessimism.

A surprising number of people in Amarillo, Texas, who
worked at the Pantex Plant, the final assembly point for all this
nation's nuclear weapons, were found to share this view. They
were supported by ministers like the Rev. Charles Jones, quoted
at the beginning of this chapter. He said things like, "Man, I get
talking about Jesus coming, it just sends chills up and down my
back." He believed in the Rapture before Armageddon: "God's
people will not be in that final battle—they'll be caught up in a
chariot of clouds to meet the Lord in the air."[12] Armageddon
theology was a particularly dangerous tangent of the Religious
Right.

## Crusading Fervor

The problem with ideologies, as we have seen, comes from
those who want to impose their particular faith on others, the
crusaders who, from left or right, insist on shaping the world according to their own vision. The ideology of nationalism, em-
braced with religious fervor, is especially troublesome. No
country can be the savior of the world. France tried it under
Napoleon, and Britain when the sun never set on its empire.
Nazi Germany embarked on a Thousand Year Reich, and the

former Soviet Union exported violence under the banner of a socialist revolution. After the Cold War it could happen with the United States taking charge of the world in the name of righteousness, interpreted as democracy and capitalism. Advocates of any ideology may be honest, sincere in their conviction that their vision is genuinely the best for all, that opponents of that vision are harming humanity. But, driven by the ideal to force it on others, they are robbing the others of their rights and thwarting their God-given aspirations. The key word here is "force." The alternative to force is sharing one's convictions by dialogue, persuasion, and example. It's important to express one's ideals because, in the words of Vatican II, "The social order requires constant improvement. It must be founded on truth, built on justice, and animated by love; in freedom it should grow every day toward a more humane balance."[13]

The social order might need constant improvement, but many "good" people are reluctant to assume responsibility for it. Some may not even be aware of such responsibility. Others may consciously or subconsciously avoid it. Fortunately for the future, a host of good people are willing to face it squarely and take up its challenge.

*If you are neutral in situations of injustice, you have chosen the side of the oppressor. If an elephant has his foot on the tail of a mouse and you say that you are neutral, the mouse will not appreciate your neutrality.*

—Bishop Desmond Tutu

CHAPTER SEVEN

# BAD FAITH AND GOOD FAITH

"The U.S. Defense Department confirmed reports that American tanks fitted with plows buried Iraqi troops alive in trenches in a key assault during the final days of the Persian Gulf War. 'There is no provision in the Geneva Convention that would prohibit this operation,' Pentagon spokesman Pete Williams said, adding, 'War is hell.'"[1]

"A young antinuclear scientist, strongly opposed to weapons work, described an experience [where] a colleague dropped in at her office one day and began to suggest how her research might have applicability to a certain kind of weapons-related work. 'We had one

of the most thrilling, exciting, and creative col-
laborative discussions I have ever had, filling pages
with diagrams and equations.' During the conversation itself, she thought only of the science at hand,
but so chagrined was she upon realizing, after he left,
how fascinated she had been with nuclear-weapons
questions that she cried bitterly for more than an
hour."[2]

THE FRENCH PHILOSOPHER Jean-Paul Sarte used the
disturbing image of "bad faith" for the efforts many "good" people make to avoid facing the unpleasant realities of their society
and the harmful consequences of their own actions. Consciously
or unconsciously, they deceive themselves about what is actually
happening. Alcoholics who deny not only to their families but
in their own mind that they drink too much are in the condition
Sartre called bad faith. So are people burdened with racism who
justify their hostility by pointing to flaws and failings in people
of another color or ethnic background.[3]

A half-century after Sartre we can admit that bad faith is
an understandable if regrettable reaction to deplorable conditions in society. It's hard enough for most of us to cope just with
the ordinary sadnesses that dot our days—a friend hospitalized,
another losing a parent to cancer, a car breakdown, humiliation
after a public mistake, an ordeal in the dentist's chair, a nagging
back pain, rumors of job layoffs. On top of that, we are deluged
with the news of more violence, hatred, suffering, indifference,
greed, and self-serving. We see starvation in Africa and ethnic
hatred in the Balkans. We hear of government cruelty in the
Middle East and of torture as official practice in Latin America.
We read about banking scandals and high-price bribery among
the business elite. We may even have a gnawing suspicion that
our own respectable professions and comfortable lifestyles are
contributing to the misery in our neighborhood or around the
world. Reading the morning paper or watching the evening

news can be a depressing experience; some sensitive people actually give up reading the paper or watching television news.

A measure of desensitization is imperative to maintain our mental balance. We have to avoid being overwhelmed by too much bleakness in these nervous times. That is not what Sartre meant by bad faith. His term, though, would apply to defense mechanisms by which "good" people whose jobs somehow contribute to the suffering of others get by. They have to avoid thinking about the suffering if they're going to be productive, if they're going to do their job well. A 20-year-old Army Ranger, home on leave, told Janice and me he was planning on studying to become an architect after completing his four-year enlistment. But in the meantime his unit was training for rapid deployment anywhere in the world. "I deliberately don't keep up on the international news," he said. "Because if we're ordered to go in someplace and do a job, I don't want to know anything about the people we'll be shooting at."

When the results are too painful to face, many "good" people just don't want to know about them. They would rather not learn about the implications of their employment, their investments, or their country's foreign policy. Their residual sense of morality, they intuitively feel, would be disturbed if they knew that automobiles they helped produce were unsafe at any speed, or the company whose stock they own has a subsidiary in Thailand that chews up children on textile machinery and dumps their bodies out on the street. They feel good about their country and want its interests defended in far-flung outposts around the world, so they don't care too much about taking a second look at history, or learning about disturbing implications of some foreign policy initiative.

The Persian Gulf War was presented as a noble triumph of courage, self-sacrifice, and technological proficiency. It was waged against what appeared to be a boastful, posturing dictator who had taken over a helpless little country in the volatile Middle East. The war seemed an exercise in American idealism coupled with American know-how. It was supposed to make us proud again of our country and our place of prominence in a new world order. After it was over, disturbing facts began to emerge into public light. National spokespersons felt they had to deny or trivialize these facts. Unfortunate by-products of our military might couldn't be allowed to dim the pride and the glory of the war itself. Some of these efforts, like shrugging off the burying alive of Iraqi soldiers because "war is hell," are clear examples of bad faith in the sense Sartre meant it. So was the refusal to keep up on international news by the young Ranger who wanted to be able to kill without feeling guilty when his unit was ordered into action.

## Avoidance Mechanisms

Earlier we looked at some of the social dynamics that create conditions causing suffering. Our focus now is on psychological devices "good" people employ to evade awareness of their involvement in these conditions. One of them is simple busyness. The tendency of "good" people, when disturbing events are on the horizon, is to concentrate on the task at hand, on doing it well, working hard at whatever is the demand of the moment. Most of us know "good" people who spend long hours on the job, then when they're at home are always fixing something around the house or building something in the basement. Or they're out shopping. They seem addicted to activity. They speak with pride about "keeping busy," about "not having enough time" to do all that they have to do. Such vigorous action can be a sign of good mental and physical health, but if it leaves no room for reflection, for understanding what's going on in the world, it's a form of bad faith.

So is an unquestioned readiness to follow someone else's orders. Many "good" people lack the inner strength to accept themselves fully and direct their own lives. Thriving under the supervision of others, they find satisfaction in accomplishing what someone else has laid out, moving in the direction someone else is pointing to. And if that direction involves mistreating the unfortunate, they go through with it, even though they would not have created such pain on their own initiative. This is the "only following orders" rationale common to those who have what psychologists call an authoritarian personality. They are comfortable only when they know that someone else is making the major decisions and telling them what to do.

The "only following orders" syndrome allows social systems whose end product is death and destruction to flourish. Richard Barnet called it the "bureaucratization of homicide." Its classic model was the elaborate network of the Holocaust, carried out largely by "good" people. Many of them were what Christopher Browning called "desk murderers." Their contribution consisted of small steps in the overall killing process, like scheduling trains, drafting legislation, sending telegrams, or compiling lists. They got up every morning, went to work, and performed their assigned tasks in a routine manner, never seeing the victims their actions affected. The bureaucratic machine was put together by others, higher up in government. Its purpose was to round up Jews all over Nazi-occupied Europe, confiscate their property, and ship them off to die in the camps. The day-to-day responsibilities of the desk murderers could be performed without confronting the reality of mass killing. But the mass killing could not have happened without their contributions.

Preoccupation with busy-ness and the ready acquiescence to authority are two common psychological mechanisms that result in a bad faith avoidance of facing full reality. Another mechanism is what psychologists call dissociation, or splitting. This is a way of blocking off one portion of the mind so that the blocked-off area may act in some degree separately from the rest of the personality. We see it in people who compartmentalize their professional life, separating it cleanly from what they do away from work. They create a nine-to-five compartment, perform efficiently when they're in it, then shut it out completely when they leave. If their job involves tax fraud in the business world or arms sales in the Third World, or if it involves promoting toxic chemicals or evicting widows and orphans, people are hurt as a result. They may regret this, but it's their job in the nine-to-five compartment. After work they try to shut the door on the compartment and get about the rest of their life in as normal a way as possible.

Such dissociation usually involves what Robert Jay Lifton called psychic numbing, a shutting down of emotions, or making a big effort to repress them, so that they won't interfere with what has to be done. "When I come to work, I'm careful to leave my feelings at the door." Professional torturers have to do this in order to keep on inflicting pain when face to face with their victims. Unfortunately, psychic numbing results in a diminished capacity to experience any emotion, often leaving a person frighteningly cold and unfeeling, like an ominous machine.

All of these ways of shutting out ugly consequences of our actions do some damage to our psyche. At best, we shove them down in our Shadow where they lie in wait to take their toll. And they don't change the reality of the ugly events one bit. They're like the Greek king who ordered the bearer of bad news to be put to death. It didn't change the bad news at all, but it provided the king with some temporary although deceptive relief. The long-range effects can be drastic. Compartmentalization and psychic numbing can lead to what is called "doubling," which carries the dissociative process further. It results in what Lifton and Markusan called "a functional second self, related to but more or less autonomous from the prior self," taking the person dangerously close to schizophrenia.[4]

## Good Faith

By contrast to mechanisms of denial, Sartre proposed "good faith" as the more difficult but more authentically human response to the unpleasant realities of our lives. Good faith is having the courage to face them squarely, acknowledging them honestly. It's what the young scientist at the beginning of this chapter showed. Despite her awareness of the atrocious nature of nuclear weapons, she was drawn into a captivating exercise of intellectual ingenuity. After her conversation about weapons was over, her essentially good faith came to the fore and prompted her toward a tearful regret.

Good faith means making a constant effort to learn the truth about ourselves, about our world, and about our selves-in-the-world. A fundamental truth about ourselves is that we are a mixed collection of good and bad components. In Charny's words, "Human beings are at one and the same time beautiful, generous, creative creatures and deadly genociders." Also, the truth about our world is that it contains, as he put it, "both a glorious epic of achievements and love and a dreadful blood-soaked nightmare of destruction."[5] The truth about our selves-in-the-world is that we have the capacity to take part in both the glorious achievements and in the blood-soaked destruction. On a less dramatic plane, our real estate friend in Chapter One had this kind of awareness when he acknowledged that he could be thought of as a slum lord.

It's hard to hold firm to the truth that human beings have the innate capacity for degradation as well as nobility. We'd rather accentuate the positive and downplay the negative. But if people who are fundamentally good and decent can succumb to one or another social imperative and become killers, at least indirectly, then I've got to keep my eyes wide open when I'm out there dealing with them. And I've got to be constantly alert to distant early warnings about holocausts and genocides. I have to be careful about myself, too. I'd better watch what I get involved in and where it might lead. It's more comforting to adopt what Martin Luther King called a "superficial optimism," to minimize the destructiveness of human affairs, or to think "things will straighten out," or that the starvation or the air strikes in the news are "really not that bad."

But evasive optimism won't do. For Thomas Aquinas, facing reality steadily is the firm foundation for the virtue of humility, which he said is solidly based on truth. It's the truth of what we ourselves are, the truth about the forces that have shaped us, the truth about our talents and accomplishments. Humility prompts us to acknowledge where we have come up short; it also allows us to take satisfaction in what we've done right. It's hard to face the truth about ourselves, to shine an exploratory light into our Shadow. It's hard to begin to untangle the subtle web of complexes we have built up to weather the slings and arrows of whatever fortunes and misfortunes we have had to face. "Know thyself" was Socrates's challenge for a lifetime.

Today we must add "know thy world" also as a lifetime challenge. What really was going on with the "ethnic cleansing" in what used to be Yugoslavia? Who really was responsible for the starvation in Somalia? What history prompted Iraq to invade Kuwait? And what was going on in Washington that influenced the U.S. decision to go to war? Searching through historical upheavals, ancient prejudices, and modern machinations is hard, but it's part of good faith.

On the other hand, to refuse to act in an emergency until we have the complete picture, what King called "the paralysis of analysis," Sartre would unhesitantly label as bad faith. At times we have to act and investigate simultaneously, then alter the actions according to what the investigation discloses.

Good faith does not come by wishing. It must be created, striven for, worked toward. And every little bit of it has to be nurtured. Western society both hinders and helps. On the one hand, society conditions us to respect and defer to authority, leading to the easy abdication of responsibility. To function efficiently any society needs the division of labor leading to bureaucratization, which lessens personal responsibility for overall outcomes and makes it easy to evade the struggle for good faith. But on the other hand, our society encourages the quest for knowledge, the curiosity and exploration that can lead to uncovering flawed results. The same society that easily accepted the military's manipulation of the media during the Gulf War encouraged the journalistic initiatives that discovered that Iraqi troops were buried alive and that tens of thousands of children died because of Iraq's crippled infrastructure. Our society respects and rewards honesty, even the painful honesty that accompanies good faith.

Because it is often painful, our stretching toward good faith requires a solid degree of personal self-esteem. We need inner strength to face the appalling facts when they appear. This strength is nourished by those personal relationships that energize us. There may be only a few people who do that for us, but associating with those from whom we receive affirmation and inspiration, and to whom we similarly contribute, is essential for developing a reliable measure of good faith. We need to help each other stay on the track.

## Choices

Good faith is the result of a decision to come down on the side of reality, no matter how unpleasant that reality might be. Making this choice involves letting go of the comfort of ignorance. It's much easier not to look at those skeleton pictures of the starving children, or the gaunt faces in detention camps. It's much easier to go a few blocks out of the way to avoid seeing the dejected figures outside the homeless mission. It's much easier to enjoy the sports page and skip the front page. Facing unpleasant reality brings about an inward discontent, because so much of the world is not right. As Flannery O'Connor said, "You shall know the truth, and the truth will make you miserable." But the misery that accompanies an eyes-open awareness is a bitter pill we have to swallow. Buddhists know it as the First Noble Truth, the truth of *dukkha*: acknowledging the pain and suffering that inevitably mar the beauty of life. Although unpleasant to contemplate and disquieting to experience, this awareness is an essential element of human wholeness. We have to pop this bitter pill if we would be whole human beings, responsible for the integrity of our lives, and responsible, too, for alleviating misery in the lives of others.

Part of the pain of good faith comes from sometimes having to choose a course of action different from others of equally good faith. Perhaps the circumstances are not clear. Never are the consequences completely known. Good people, acting in whatever measure of good faith they achieve, can differ seriously with each other. Many good people, with a large measure of good faith, are strongly opposed to abortion and press for legislation outlawing it. Many others, with an equally large measure of good faith, are in favor of a woman's right to make this agonizing personal choice without being treated as a criminal.

Further, good faith, even if it could be achieved all around, does not assure harmony. Areas of disagreement abound. What role ought punishment to have in a family or society? How do we balance the need for a growing economy with the need to preserve the environment? Many in good faith favor the use of violence to defend themselves, their families, and their country. Many others, in equally good faith, oppose the use of such violence, and advocate conscientious objection to military service, strict gun control legislation, and international disarmament.

But whenever violence is a good faith choice, it is always a reluctant one. Good faith leads to what theology professor David Ray Griffin called a "pacific mentality." Such a mentality is not necessarily absolutist in rejecting all violence. But it's an attitude that "naturally wants and seeks peaceful solutions to conflicts, a mentality that loathes violence and would only resort to it, if at all, in extreme circumstances."[6] Life is spotted with hurt. Sometimes it's the result of a deliberate choice that has to be made between the lesser of two evils, for example, injuring an attacker to prevent a rape, or taking a serious business loss instead of laying off employees. We can't eliminate it, but we can diminish it. Recognizing this challenge is a necessary component of good faith.

Most of us will only partially achieve a good faith response to the mixed-up realities of life. Few will reach the purity of a Gandhi or King or Dorothy Day or Daniel Berrigan. Most of us will struggle for our integrity. We may doggedly go through the morning paper, but some days we'll spend more time on the entertainment section than on the international news. On the road we'll come across an automobile accident, take a quick glance to see if any victims are visible, but not stop to investigate further because we're hurrying to an appointment. The integrity of total good faith is a condition few of us will reach. But we can hope to be on the right track, bolstered by the conviction that the cosmos, with all its flaws and dangers, is, on balance, benign. "The arc of the moral universe is long," King liked to say, "but it bends toward justice."

For Sartre, the acid test of good faith is what we *do* with our awareness. To be authentic is to attempt to do something about one's necessary participation in evil other than experiencing its tragedy. What we do needs to be in the direction of changing ourselves and changing our world for the better. But this mandate is too broad to be helpful. Sartre gave it a very specific focus. Authentic persons, people of good faith, he said, "always align themselves as much as possible with the most disadvantaged members of a community." To help them takes more than good-faith understanding; it takes the quality of compassion, the gift we will consider next.

*A universal love is not only psychologically possible; it is the only complete and final way in which we are able to love.*

—Teilhard de Chardin

# CHAPTER EIGHT

# THE GIFT OF COMPASSION

"The other day in the midst of Port-au-Prince I saw a car, an old battered car, a jalopy, falter and sputter and come to a slow halt. The man who was driving the car got out and looked at it, stuck there in the middle of traffic, helpless. Then I saw another face, the passenger. A woman. The driver looked around the street at the unemployed loungers who are always there, and said to them, 'She is going to have a baby right here. If we do not get to the hospital, she will die. Her baby will die, too.' The loungers looked at the car and heard the man's voice and saw the woman's tears. Their backs straightened, their cigarettes fell to the ground, their eyes cleared. They approached the car, eight of them, leaned over, and put their shoulders to the chore. Down one long dusty road, a left turn, and down another, through the green and white gates of the State Hospital, and she had arrived."[1]

"The first big street round-up took place in Amsterdam and voluntarily Etty decided to go with the trapped Jews to Westerbork. She did not want to escape the fate of the Jewish people. She believed that she could do justice to life only if she did not abandon those in danger, and if she used her strength to bring light into the life of others. Survivors from the camp have confirmed that Etty was a 'luminous' personality to the last."[2]

As GOOD FAITH MEANS adequate awareness, action to right the wrongs springs from compassionate caring. The word "love" has been so overused that it seems too trite for the wellspring of caring that drives people to hold out a helping hand. Compassion, whose ancient Latin root means "suffering with," is a different way of speaking about love. It connotes sympathetic understanding, a sense of what's going on under the surface, emerging as a desire to alleviate some of the pain. Sensitivity to the hurts that are being felt by others, the harm that is being inflicted in every direction we look, spurs us into exerting ourselves in helpful and healing ways.

Compassion is the solidarity with the trapped Jews in Amsterdam that compelled Etty Hillesum, in the quote above, to give up her freedom and accompany them to the concentration camp, knowing that it might well mean her own death. Compassion is the readiness to come to the aid of a helpless woman in Haiti and push her disabled car to the hospital.

Something about the cold detachment of a person who looks on the suffering of others and turns away unaffected is repelling. Too much desensitization creates accomplices to atrocity. In his novel *Beyond the Wall*, Elie Wiesel described a concentration camp survivor who is jolted by the memory of an impassive face in a window who had watched the deportation of Jews with no sign of emotion. The survivor reflects:

> This, this was the thing I had wanted to understand ever since the war. Nothing else. How a human being can remain indifferent. The executioners I understood; also the victims, though with more difficulty. For the others, all the others, those who were neither for nor against, those who sprawled in passive patience, those who told themselves, "The storm will blow over and everything will be normal again," those who thought themselves above the battle, those who were permanently and merely spectators—all those were closed to me, incomprehensible.[3]

In Wiesel's novel the survivor, Michael, meets that spectator when he goes back to visit his village after the war. Michael is appalled when he realizes that the man still has no sense of concern, even after the gruesome events of the camps have been revealed. He discovers, to his surprise, that he cannot hate the spectator. All he can feel is contempt.

Fifty years after the Holocaust we've made progress in understanding the executioners who perpetrated the atrocities. We've seen what there is in the shadowy depths of the human spirit and the compelling pressures of social conformity that pushed some, like the ordinary men of the Hamburg police battalion, into this role. We've also come to know about the dissociation and psychic numbing that allowed others to fill the less vicious but still deadly role of desk murderers, or passive spectators.

Not everyone in that degrading era under the Nazi spell was an executioner or cooperator or passive spectator. Some, like Etty Hillesum of Amsterdam, actively stepped in to help the victims. Our hope for a better future will be more firmly grounded when we know as much about people like Etty and why they did what they did as we know about the Nazi criminals who devised the genocidal program, and about the ordinary people who carried it out, or just stood by and let it happen.

## Rescuers

The earliest attention after the war concentrated on the perpetrators of the Holocaust and cooperators. It was only later that interest in those who intervened to help during those dark days became more widespread. Rescuers, like most of the perpetrators, cooperators, and spectators, were themselves ordinary people. Some were farmers, others teachers, still others had small businesses or worked in factories. Some were wealthy, others poor. They were not distinguished by their religious background or marital status. Very few were larger-than-life heroes, even in retrospect. One study in the 1980s, based on interviews with hundreds of men and women who, at great personal risk, aided Jews in hiding or escaping, found that such people had what psychologists call "altruistic personalities."

Certain common factors were found in the family background and personality profile of those who came forward when it was most needed and despite severe odds. They had received from their families two significant values. One was a fundamental sense of decency in dealing with others: honesty, generosity, and respect. "I learned to be good to one's neighbor, honesty, scruples—to be responsible, concerned, and considerate," was the way one woman put it. She said she learned "to work—and work hard. But also to help—to the point of leaving one's work to help one's neighbor."[4] The other key value was the widespread extent of that decency, that it should go out to all people, not just to those who were close at hand. "[My father] taught me to love my neighbor—to consider him my equal whatever his nationality or religion," said another, matter-of-factly. "[My mother] taught me to be responsible, honest, to respect older people, to respect all people—not to tease or criticize people of other religions," responded a third.[5]

The war in Europe created intense anxieties for personal survival. Rescuers worried like everyone else about food, shelter, and protection for themselves and their families. They did not noticeably lack such self-concern. Nor did they disregard the approval of others. Rescuers, like cooperators, were very aware of what others thought of them. But, despite this pressure, they acted differently from their neighbors because of their strong sense of responsibility for others' welfare, and the wide extent of that responsibility.

## Road-to-Damascus Jolts

For some ordinary Europeans who intervened to help, an extraordinary event like the wholesale round-up of Jews activated their compassion. It brought to the fore their vivid sense of connectedness, and their determination to do something about it. Similar life-enlightening experiences have jolted other people, in other times and places, into a similar commitment.

It happened to nuclear weapons physicist Theodore Taylor during his first visit to what was then the Soviet Union. As a planner for the Pentagon, he had been extensively involved in determining which bombs with which megatonnage would be appropriate for which targets within the city of Moscow. Now, standing in Red Square himself, he observed many young people in wedding parties visiting Lenin's tomb, and was impressed by how happy they looked. Suddenly something snapped. He began weeping uncontrollably. "It was seeing those happy-looking, specific people going around, working their way up to the mausoleum," he later said. "For any human being to contemplate setting off a bomb on top of this, these people, is a symptom of insanity."[6] When he returned home, Taylor resigned his position with the government.

An unexpected encounter with human horror had a similar life-changing effect on Mother Teresa. In August 1946 she was a young sister teaching in a sheltered girls' school in Calcutta when the city erupted in a Hindu-Muslim bloodbath. It became known as the Day of the Great Killing. Because she was head-mistress, Sr. Teresa had to go outside the convent in search of food for her students. She later described it to a friend.

> I had three hundred girls in the boarding school and we had nothing to eat. We were not supposed to go out into the streets, but I went anyway. Then I saw the bodies on the streets, stabbed, beaten, lying there in strange positions in their dried blood. We had been behind our safe walls. We knew that there had been rioting. People had been jumping over our walls, first a Hindu, then a Muslim....When I went out on the street—only then I saw the death that was fol-lowing them.[7]

Less than a month later, traveling to her annual retreat, Teresa was inspired by what she felt was a message from Jesus. "It was on that train that I heard the call to give up all and follow Him into the slums—to serve Him in the poorest of the poor. I knew it was His will and that I had to follow Him." The call, shortly after her shock on the Day of the Great Killing, led her into a career of compassion that culminated in her receiving, in 1979, the Nobel Peace Prize—and the respect of the world.

Another person jolted into a similar change of direction was the monk Thomas Merton. From his secluded cell inside a Trappist monastery in rural Kentucky, Merton's writings touched the minds and hearts of millions with his compas-sionate sensitivity. But he hadn't always felt that way. He had entered the monastery in 1941 on a personal spiritual quest, which to him meant isolation, separation from the world's swirl. After a time of soothing solitude, there came a moment in his life when everything unexpectedly changed. It happened when he was forty miles away from his cloister on an errand in the city. He described it in his journal:

> Yesterday, in Louisville, at the corner of 4th and
> Walnut, I suddenly realized that I loved all the people
> and that none of them were, or could be, totally alien
> to me. As if waking from a dream—the dream of my
> separateness, of my "special" vocation to be differ-
> ent....I am still a member of the human race—and
> what more glorious destiny is there, since the Word
> was made flesh and became, too, a member of the
> Human Race![8]

# How to Get There

One doesn't have to be a Thomas Merton or Mother
Teresa to come alive with compassion. Everyone is capable of it.
We see it exhibited in the spontaneous outpouring of generosity
at times of natural disasters, as in the San Francisco earthquake
in 1989 or the devastation of South Florida by hurricane
Andrew in 1992. We even recognize compassion in the pro-
verbial contract killer who loves his aged mother, or the cynical
stripper who nurses her sick baby, or the fleecing financier who
secretly supports a homeless shelter.

The Chinese communist government tried for years to in-
still a sense of compassion in young children. They called it al-
truism in the interest of society, but the goal was the same:
sensitivity to the needs of others and a willingness to extend a
helping hand. One such effort was described to me by a
University of Arkansas professor who had visited a Chinese
classroom. On the front wall of the room was a series of four posters. The first showed a little girl and boy together, but the boy
had inadvertently dropped his handkerchief. In the second
poster the little girl picks up the handkerchief. The third shows
her at home carefully ironing it, and in the fourth she gives it
back to the little boy. The children in that classroom would be
absorbing the selfless message of those posters all day long.

Siddhartha Gautama, the Buddha, was one of the world's greatest teachers of compassion. He got the message across in different ways. One is illustrated in the beloved Buddhist story of Kisa Gotami. She was a young woman whose newborn child had died.

> In her grief she carried the dead child to all her neighbors, asking them for medicine, and the people said: "She has lost her senses. The boy is dead." At length Kisa Gotami met a man who replied to her request: "I cannot give thee medicine for thy child, but I know a physician who can." And the girl said: "Pray tell me, sir; who is it?" And the man replied: "Go to Sakyamuni, the Buddha."
>
> Kisa Gotami repaired to the Buddha and cried: "Lord and Master, give me the medicine that will cure my boy." The Buddha answered: "I want a handful of mustard-seed." And when the girl in her joy promised to procure it, the Buddha added: "The mustard-seed must be taken from a house where no one has lost a child, husband, parent, or friend."
>
> Poor Kisa Gotami now went from house to house, and the people pitied her and said: "Here is mustard-seed; take it!" But when she asked, "Did a son or daughter, a father or mother, die in your family?" they answered her: "Alas! the living are few, but the dead are many. Do not remind us of our deepest grief." And there was no house but some beloved one had died in it.
>
> Kisa Gotami became weary and hopeless, and sat down at the wayside, watching the lights of the city, as they flickered up and were extinguished again. At last the darkness of the night reigned everywhere. And she considered the fate of human beings, that their lives flicker up and are extinguished. And she

thought to herself: "How selfish am I in my grief! Death is common to all; yet in this valley of desolation there is a path that leads him to immortality who has surrendered all selfishness."

Putting away the selfishness of her affection for her child, Kisa Gotami had the dead body buried in the forest. Returning to the Buddha, she took refuge in him and found comfort in the Dharma, which is a balm that will soothe all the pains of our troubled hearts.[9]

Under the Buddha's gentle guidance, Kisa Gotami was able to rise above her self-centered grief, understandable and necessary as it was, and begin to feel an other-centered compassion.

We can look at the individual lives of those who exhibit compassion and find supportive family closeness, or road-to-Damascus eye-openers, or a mature loving companionship. But others exposed to these same influences may never develop altruistic personalities. To some extent, compassion can be taught, as with Kisa Gotami stories, or the Chinese poster series. But the children who listen to the stories or absorb the poster lesson don't always grow up to be compassionate adults. Why some people acquire it and some don't is still not fully known. Medieval theologians spoke of "infused virtues," of "grace," of "gratuitous gifts from God," neither deserved by personal merit nor acquired by personal effort. The inner energy of compassion so necessary to heal the wounds and nurture the world is still mysterious. The medieval theological categories continue to be relevant in giving a symbol for the mystery.

## Compassion Blockers

As we consider ways compassion is acquired, it helps to look also at some of the formidable obstacles in its way. The intense nationalism that seems to be taking on a new life in the closing years of this century is one obstacle. It is rooted in tribal

instincts that have been around a long time. People need to feel
the closeness and support of kindred spirits. Tribalism says to
love your neighbor, but don't let your love go beyond the neighborhood. Tribalism carries with it a fear of the "other," the out-
sider who would threaten our special arrangement, upset our
apple cart. This fear can lead to hatred and overt violence
against the outsiders. We see it in the continued Hindu-Muslim
bloodshed in South Asia. We are saddened by the tenacious
Catholic-Protestant feud in Northern Ireland, and the black-
white hatred in Southern Africa. Nationalism was an ingredient
in the ugly "ethnic cleansing" in parts of the former Yugoslavia.
And it pumped up the fury of that Desert Storm that killed tens
of thousands of Iraqis, burying some alive and condemning others to slow death from disease. Sometimes a tribal hatred against
outsiders is even promoted by calculating leaders who sense that
it supplies a cement for the society.

A second contemporary compassion blocker is the heightened individualism that draws the boundaries of love even further in. In the United States it is rooted in the frontier
mythology and the personal-salvation stress in American religion, which we looked at earlier. It is unfortunately all too
widespread where people have achieved a high level of technological proficiency. One of its sources is a production system
that is organized for maximum efficiency. Persons with specialized skills perform functions that interlock with other specialized
functions. Although differing personalities are taken into con-
sideration by sophisticated managers, the overall feeling is that
everyone is expected to function smoothly as parts of the machine. An emphasis on Total Quality Management tries to ensure maximum effectiveness at every level of the operation.

Those who become absorbed in such a system experience
on-the-job depersonalization. Having to function as gears in a
process that becomes as predictable as possible prompts a com-
pensatory reaction away from work. A sense of powerlessness
turns them inward to the only area they intuitively sense they

can control, the self. They tend to express themselves, and reach for a degree of personal fulfillment, by highly individualistic expressions of clothing, style, musical tastes, and recreational preferences. They feel vulnerable, and have to build their personal fortifications. If they do things with others, it is often in shared experiences of self-expression, such as dancing separately together, or listening to music so loud they cannot have even a pretense of conversation. Their need is to take care of themselves first, and often exclusively. It's no coincidence that the Sony Walkman radio, which provides private entertainment in the midst of a crowd, was invented in Japan, a society of even more pervasive technological proficiency than the United States. Such self-preoccupation blocks attention to others and reduces one's ability to recognize others' needs. In the best of times, self-interest guides much of our behavior. In high-tech times it can be all-consuming.

A third major obstacle to compassion is the incessant stress that presses in on far too many and that seems to be escalating endlessly. A friend of Janice's and mine in the newly independent Ukraine was able to obtain a small patch of land on which to plant some vegetables. He told us he and his family would survive the harsh winter no matter what, because despite the barren grocery shelves he would have enough potatoes in the cellar to make it through until spring. Many skilled workers in the industrialized West also suffer economic anxiety, not from a harsh winter and barren stores, but from the fear of a collapsing house of monetary cards that will leave them floundering for life support. They realize they don't have anything in the cellar to see them through that kind of winter. The desperation to keep what they already have pushes them toward conflict rather than compassion.

Stress also comes from the incessant images on the television screen. Dozens of channels, hundreds with a satellite dish, promise ever more interesting sights and sounds. They portray a kaleidoscopic world baffling by its elusiveness until we figure out its ephemeral nature and ease away from its allure. Otherwise we're victimized by it. And we feel alone in our victimization because others are experiencing the same stress but from a different mix of images. They're flipping through different channels than we are, and are trying to cope with their own resultant unease.

## Species Consciousness

But there's a silver lining to some of these clouds. The same technological proficiency that fosters a heightened individualism paradoxically provides the means of achieving a new level of global solidarity. With the world wired together in what is practically an intercontinental television network, we can learn about events in a distant part of the world as they are happening. The television lights and cameras that surprised the Navy Seals coming ashore on Somalia's beaches showed their landing to the whole world as it was taking place. Skin-head violence against immigrants in Germany seems as close as gang violence in California. Celebratory fireworks over Washington at President Clinton's inauguration ceremonies were juxtaposed uneasily with anti-aircraft fireworks over Baghdad the same evening. We have entered the era of what Lifton and Markusan called "species consciousness."

> Whatever the capacity of an individual self for concern, caring, loyalty, and even love can now be extended in some degree to the human species as a whole....However flawed and partial, the species self is likely to advocate moral and political policies attuned not to only a single group or nation but to all humankind.[10]

Whether or not we agree that such universal advocacy is "likely," we see that it is possible to an unprecedented degree.

Gandhi had anticipated it much earlier: "My goal is friendship with the whole world." Decades ago, Teilhard de Chardin wrote, "The age of nations is past. The task before us now, if we would not perish, is to shake off our ancient prejudices, and to build the earth." When we get beyond the blinders of nationalism and the restraints of individualism, we find ourselves in a strange and beautiful landscape, where once familiar landmarks take on a different hue, and once strange and forbidding areas suddenly become familiar. When we become acclimated to this new vision, we will never be able to go back again to our old ghettos.

The more one takes in this awesome global scenery, the more one becomes aware of the interdependence of all human beings. We feel an expansion of the self, knowing the need to extend ourselves in serving, in caring, in forgiving. Our life has been elevated to a higher level. How it got there we may not know with certainty, but, grateful for the gift, we can set about doing genuinely good things.

> *They ask me sometimes, and mean well by it, "How of-*
> *ten have you been arrested?" But I dislike the numbers*
> *game, and turn the question aside with: "As yet, not*
> *enough."*
>
> —Daniel Berrigan

# CHAPTER NINE

# GOOD PEOPLE
# DOING GOOD THINGS

"The city lights twinkle far below Jim Brown's home, steam rises from his heated swimming pool and the boys from the 'hood sit in his living room awaiting their weekly dose of self-esteem. The 55-year-old football Hall of Famer greets each of them with the smooth, grip-shifting handshake of the streets. They call him Mr. Brown. He gives them free run of the house, lets them raid his refrigerator, play his stereo, swim in the pool. For the last year, these reunions have been the soul of Brown's latest project, a 15-step course in personal responsibility he calls The Amer-I-Can Program of positive thought, proper communication, goal-setting, family relationships and job-seeking skills."[1]

"Cesar Chavez has said that a national campaign will succeed if only ten or eleven percent of the people support it. Changing the world, in other words, requires the assistance (or resistance) not of every single person, but of a conscientious, committed minority. The United Farm Workers, as with civil rights and similar movements around the world, requires, also, a disciplined, faithful leadership. Chavez, recently deceased, used to fast periodically. 'The fast is the heartfelt prayer for purification and strengthening for all of us,' he said."[2]

QUICKENED BY THE GIFT of compassion, we can direct our energies in ways that make a constructive difference in the world. While we continue our inward struggle toward good faith, we can extend an outward hand to those in need at the moment. Sometimes the opportunity is thrust upon us, as it was to the Samaritan on the road to Jericho. It could happen on our way to work, suddenly shocked when a driver runs a red light and smashes into an innocent car. At other times we can make a conscious effort to help those we know are hurting. We reach out to someone hungry or sick or homeless or grief-stricken, giving the cup of cold water that Jesus and Mohammed both praised.

Hospitality starts at home, advice most of us received years ago. Our first compassionate concern has to be to the immediate needs of those Dietrich Bonhoeffer called "the nearest Thou at hand"—our family first, then those with whom we are associated in the neighborhood and workplace. The social activist or civic do-gooder who neglects family or neighbors in the interests of the

Big Picture, who is constantly focusing on the horizon and doesn't see the ground directly below, may in fact be avoiding something personally difficult. It's sometimes easier to wrestle with problems in the abstract than engage the complexities of real living and breathing human beings in front of us. They can be messy and discomforting. But if they're hurting, and if we're whole enough to help, their need demands our attention. The Big Picture can wait.

Caring for the nearest Thou at hand can at times be all-consuming. Raising small children is. So is nursing an invalid parent, or helping resolve a neighborhood crisis. When this pressure eases, opportunities and needs beyond our immediate environment abound. What we do doesn't have to be dramatic; it doesn't have to solve the problem. An early ad for the Peace Corps proclaimed a modest aim: "Not to change the world, but not to leave it the same, either." Whatever good we do may not be noticed, may not elicit a grateful response. But the important thing is that we are reversing the vector of our energy from self-serving to other-serving. We are bringing a bit of healing into the lives of others.

## Direct Help

Hale House in Harlem, a place of refuge for babies with AIDS or drug-abusing parents, was the outgrowth of the compassionate concern of an elderly woman. She decided to devote her later years to caring for the most fragile victims of New York City's tragic epidemics. Clara Hale was 63 years old and retired when she took into her home a two-month-old infant whose drug-addicted mother allowed the baby to slip out of her arms as she nodded off in a stupor on the sidewalk. When Clara Hale died in 1992, at 87, the house she started had cared for hundreds of children and helped rehabilitate many of their parents.[3]

In the Philippines, Janice and I met a slim, vivacious young woman named Pearlie, who had helped found an organization called the Center of Unity. We met her in the city of Olongapo, next to the U.S. naval base at Subic Bay. For years Pearlie had been what was politely called a "hospitality woman." As a waitress in an Olongapo bar she was one of the many prostitutes serving the American sailors who flocked by the thousands into the city when their ships docked at Subic. Pearlie had come to Olongapo in the hopes of making a little money—enough to live on, enough to send some back to her impoverished family. When we met her, she was working full-time for the Center of Unity, providing companionship and counseling for women who had become trapped in the spiral of sex and drugs and abortion. The Center helped many of Olongapo's hospitality women extricate themselves from that degrading spiral in the years before the United States closed the base.

Former football star Jim Brown developed his self-help program in Los Angeles to change the outlook of deprived young black men in that troubled city. His efforts had a ripple effect on others crippled by poverty and racism. Like Pearlie reaching out to improve the lives of abused women in the Philippines, Jim Brown reached out to improve the lives of hurting men in Los Angeles. Clara Hale also made a difference with her care for helpless babies and many of their parents in Harlem. All three of these good samaritans, and myriad others around the world who feed the hungry, shelter the homeless, and comfort the victims of violence, are good people doing good things.

## Structural Change

Compassionate action is necessary on another level also. Improving education systems, health care delivery, and employment opportunities will benefit a larger number of people in a longer run. Martin Luther King directed attention to this level of involvement with his image of the Jericho Road Improvement Association. By improving safety along the road, we help many more travelers get to their destination with their health and purse intact. Robert McAfee Brown defined peacemaking as the spreading of _shalom_, enhancing the well-being of the human family. When he described peacemaking as "action to alleviate world hunger, including that down the block," he was pointing to the two areas in which our other-serving energies can be directed. One is immediate need: the hunger down the block. It is the Salvation Army giving a bed for a night. It is a soup kitchen providing a meal to whoever shows up. The other area is, like the Jericho Road Improvement Association, action on a broader scale to alleviate hunger: lobbying to change discriminatory laws, demonstrating to stop an immoral war.

The large social protests of the 1960s were classic examples of the second. The Civil Rights Movement, quietly at first, then with increasing public visibility, brought to the attention of the entire country the systematic deprivation of rights suffered by African-Americans in the south. King understood how direct-action tactics could stimulate corrective national legislation. The famous Selma to Montgomery march in the spring of 1965 dramatized that dynamic. Attempts to walk from Selma were met at first with trampling horses and the clubs of state troopers. Shortly afterwards, as hundreds of participants gathered from around the country, and as television cameras showed the world what was happening, federal troops escorted the marchers along the trek to the Alabama state capitol. The march led directly to strong voting rights legislation enacted by an impressed Congress. When President Lyndon Johnson signed the bill, he publicly acknowledged the effectiveness of the movement:

> The real hero of this struggle is the American Negro. His actions and protests, his call to risk safety, and even risk his life, have awakened the conscience of this nation. His demonstrations have been designed to call attention to injustice; designed to stir reform.[4]

The largely nonviolent outpourings of public witness in the Civil Rights Movement helped improve the lives of millions of African-Americans not only in the south but throughout the country.

Similar tactics characterized the peace movement that dominated the second half of the 1960s. Men and women by the tens of thousands took risks and interrupted the routine of their lives to voice their belief that the U.S. should end its involvement in Vietnam. Never before in the history of this country had opposition to a war been so widespread. As in the Civil Rights Movement, acts of civil disobedience characterized resistance to the Vietnam War. One of the more startling was the burning of draft files that were the property of the government. Daniel Berrigan and his brother Philip led the first of these actions in Catonsville, Maryland, outside Baltimore. His trial testimony gave eloquent expression to the fervent desire for an end to the war:

> We shall beyond doubt be placed behind bars for some portion of our natural lives in consequence of our inability to live and die content in the plagued city, to say "peace, peace" when there is no peace, to keep the poor poor, the thirsty and hungry thirsty and hungry. Our apologies, good friends, for the fracture of good order, the burning of paper instead of children, the angering of the orderlies in the front parlor of the charnel house. We could not, so help us God, do otherwise.[5]

The public outcry of millions of others who, like the Berrigans, could not do otherwise under the specter of that war, pressed people in power in government. The national administration in Washington changed its course. They first stopped the war's escalation, then withdrew American troops from Vietnam, and finally ended American support for the war altogether. The peace movement saved the lives of many thousands of Americans and Vietnamese who would have died in that protracted, unwinnable combat.

The United Farm Workers in California, under the leadership of Cesar Chavez, quoted at the beginning of this chapter, adopted large-scale nonviolent protest tactics from Gandhi and King, and succeeded in improving working conditions for thousands of neglected and often exploited agricultural workers. The great social movements of the 1960s confirmed for a generation of Americans the effectiveness of such tactics. They showed that sustained public campaigns channeling compassionate concern could indeed better the lives of a large number of people. If it took organizing mass marches, getting arrested for disobeying unjust laws to call attention to labor abuse, people like King and the Berrigans and Cesar Chavez, and thousands of others, would continue to do it—until social conditions improved.

Janice and I admired Pearlie in the Philippines for giving direct help to the victims of military sexual abuse. We also admired people we met there who were working in another way. Among them were the idealistic men and women in the Manila office of the Nuclear-Free Philippines Coalition. They were organizing political leadership and galvanizing public opinion for the removal of the U.S. bases altogether. Theirs was another way of trying to relieve the misery of the tens of thousands of hospitality women. Both direct help and structural change are important. Neither should be viewed as the exclusive "right" thing to do. Both are needed to improve the lives of those who are suffering.

Two quite different organizations in Memphis, Tennessee, where Janice and I live, illustrate the two approaches. Both involve good people working together to do many good things. One, the Metropolitan Inter-Faith Association, MIFA, is a model of direct help. The other, the Mid-South Peace and Justice Center, works for structural change.

## Metropolitan Inter-Faith Association

Almost everyone in Memphis knows MIFA. Over the past quarter of a century it has helped tens of thousands of people to survive emergencies and get back on their feet. MIFA did not start out as a direct-help agency. In early 1968 a few clergy and lay religious leaders met to explore cooperation across denominational lines to meet some of the growing social needs in Memphis. It was a time when established ways of doing things, politics as usual, were being called into question throughout the country. New possibilities seemed limitless. Optimism was high. Those who met that first time were gratified by their shared concern, new to a city with deep-seated religious and racial differences. They didn't know exactly what they could do, but they wanted to do something. They chose Metropolitan Inter-Faith Association as their name, and agreed to meet again.

Unexpectedly, one might say providentially, an event took place a few days later that was to have history-changing repercussions. In February 1968, the city's sanitation workers went on strike. They had been asking for better wages, better working conditions, and recognition for their union. When negotiation attempts with city officials were repeatedly rebuffed, they decided to strike. Because the workers were almost entirely black and the city administration almost entirely white, the strike quickly became a racial confrontation. Hostility and bitterness filled the Memphis air, along with the odor of rotting garbage. The strikers turned to Martin Luther King for help.

When King received the request, he agreed to intervene. In effect, he said, he could not do otherwise. "The question is not, if I stop to help this man in need, what will happen to me? The question is, if I do not stop to help the sanitation workers, what will happen to them?"[6]

King came to Memphis and the workers marched. Tension grew throughout the city. National Guard troops were called out to keep order. When the strike was not settled and King came back in April to lead another march, he was killed. The day after his assassination, with the city in emotional turmoil and national guard troops on full alert, a contingent of religious leaders, most of whom had been involved in starting MIFA, walked in solemn procession from the Episcopal Cathedral to City Hall to see the mayor. Their action led to an eventual settlement of the strike.

Born in crisis and nurtured by the desire to carry on King's dream, the new organization of MIFA faced distrust by those opposed to changing the city's old ways. MIFA's supporters found the going tenuous and rocky. Its detractors took to calling it MAFIA.

Since early efforts at community organizing met with little success, MIFA's leaders shifted course. Putting aside its original impetus for social change, MIFA began to fulfill King's dream in another way: organizing direct services to the needy. This was to be its permanent identity. With the help of a federal grant, MIFA's first successful venture was a program to carry senior citizens to congregate meal sites in cooperating church facilities. Within a short time, MIFA also began a Meals on Wheels program to deliver food to shut-ins. In the early months, volunteers supplied their own cars for both operations. MIFA's transportation arm gradually expanded to a fleet of sixty vehicles. By the early 1990s, Meals on Wheels had reached a level of over 100 volunteers delivering more than 3000 hot meals each day.

MIFA developed a Food Bank with resources from local companies and private contributions, which grew to the capacity of distributing 2.5 million pounds of food a year to over 150 community agencies. At the beginning of the 1990s MIFA's 44 Food Pantries were providing three-day supplies for 20,000 needy families a year. Its Emergency Services included helping with rent, food, clothing, and housing for the elderly, the critically ill, and the handicapped, those most in need.

And still MIFA grew, carefully stewarding its resources. It offered disadvantaged young people the chance to earn their first paychecks and start planning their careers through community service summer jobs and after-school work. MIFA enlisted the cooperation of Memphis Light, Gas and Water to encourage customers to authorize an extra dollar added to their monthly bills. MIFA then administered those donated dollars for utilities and weatherizing assistance to families in crisis.

With financial help from the city, MIFA built 25 small houses to provide temporary living for people without resources. They could stay in these houses for up to a year, while MIFA supplied job training, child care, and education assistance. With this help, dozens of formerly homeless people found new life, equipped with new skills and renewed self-esteem.

Twenty-five years after its first uncertain beginnings, MIFA had grown to a staff of over 200 people administering 32 different programs. It served 8000 people in four counties—two in Tennessee, one across the Mississippi River in Arkansas, and the other over the city's southern border in Mississippi. Many of the staff were volunteers. Others were paid professionals willing to work for less than their counterparts in public or other private agencies. Its funding came from a variety of sources, including contributions from churches and synagogues, grants from federal, county, and city governments, and private foundations. It had become a solidly established and highly respected contributor to the quality of life in the Memphis area. MIFA defined its continued aim as "self-help for the able, support services for the frail, and emergency services for those in crisis."

## Mid-South Peace and Justice Center

By contrast with direct help, which can be directly rewarding, most of the work for structural change is tedious, behind-the-scenes, and thankless in lacking immediate results. Those who doggedly keep at it are motivated by the realization that a large number of people can lead more humane lives if crippling conditions—an international arms race or toxic waste dumping—are abolished. They can also be helped if enabling measures such as non-discriminatory lending practices or comprehensive health care legislation are enacted. The aim of the Mid-South Peace and Justice Center was to encourage such enabling measures and remove crippling conditions. It was founded on the conviction that peace involves a social foundation of justice, and that the process of justice demands ceaseless vigilance and grass-roots activism.

A Memphis-based peace and justice center was "a ship that needs to be built." These words of a Baptist minister summed up the reaction of some thirty concerned women and men who gathered in June 1981 at a local Catholic college to discuss a proposal for such a center. The immediate aim was to free up several people from other professional responsibilities. They could then devote their full energies to peace and social justice activities in the city and surrounding areas, the region known as Mid-South. Effective work for structural change needed to be consistently planned and centrally organized. That took time and energy beyond what could be expected from volunteers. It called for a staff and an office.

With the support of key members of the city's religious and academic communities, the Center opened on January 15, 1982. Because the initial support was more moral than monetary, the Center began on a wing and a prayer. The wing was $600 contributed by a local tax resister, plus a talented young staff person willing to raise money for her salary and work part-time as an auto mechanic until more ample funds came. The prayers flowered in the enthusiasm of more than a dozen volunteers who gave of their time and talents to restore and paint an office, serve on a policy-making board, set up a computerized mailing list, and help organize the Center's first actions. Martin Luther King's birthday was chosen for the formal opening, because those who believed in his dream saw the Center as carrying on his work—much like MIFA's original founders had felt fourteen years earlier.

The Center from the beginning had two essential characteristics. Its spirit was nonviolent, in the active way of Gandhi and King. And, although it was not identified with any church or religious group, it was faith-based and not purely secular. Its *raison d'etre* was set forth in a mission statement:

As people of faith, we are inspired by hope for a just society within a just global order. We are actively implementing a vision for our community and the world marked by enduring peace that results from economic, political and social justice. The Center works by utilizing a variety of personal gifts and collective means to help individuals and groups to educate and empower themselves for participatory change in national, state and local policies in a common spirit of nonviolence.

Its work was carried on through task forces of volunteers from the community, coordinated by staff professionals. To use its modest resources as effectively as possible, the Center concentrated on four priorities:

1. Disarmament, with emphasis on banning the testing of nuclear weapons and eventually eliminating them altogether, and redirecting the national budget away from military spending toward meeting human needs.

2. Central America, because of the deep trouble plaguing that tortured region since the Center's inception. The Center coordinated informational resources and speakers. It also organized efforts to encourage legislation that would lower the level of violence in El Salvador, Guatemala, and, during the 1980s especially, Nicaragua.

3. South Africa, with its cruel apartheid and uncertain future. The Center held workshops and provided knowledgeable people to speak in schools and churches. It called attention to the boycott of products and companies that supported the South African government. It organized a sister-community arrangement between the Memphis city government and a black township outside Port Elizabeth in South Africa.

4. Local Issues, such as lack of affordable housing for many, discriminatory policies of lending institutions, and toxic waste dumps in poverty areas. Through calling attention to these abus-

es and pressing for corrective legislation, it set in motion many healing processes.

During the Center's first decade its accomplishments included publicizing the transport of nuclear weapons through the heart of the city. In the mid-1980s the Center made national news by alerting people to passage through Memphis of the White Train. Twice a year a specially designed train carried nuclear bombs from the Pantex plant in Amarillo, Texas, to the Charleston Navy Yard in South Carolina and the Kings Bay Trident submarine base in Georgia. Some of the Center's staff and associates were arrested for blocking the railroad tracks. When the Department of Energy stopped using the train and began transporting the bombs in truck convoys, the Center tracked and followed the trucks on Interstate 40 in east Arkansas and west Tennessee, through the city of Memphis. The publicity such actions generated helped influence local public opinion, which lent support to efforts at securing nuclear disarmament agreements between the United States and the former Soviet Union.

The Center's work helped people in Central America also. At a time when paramilitary groups in the Mid-South were providing weapons and logistical support for the Nicaraguan contras, the Center did the tough, basic research and education to bring an alternative message on Central America to school, church, and civic groups. In this way it kept the Contra war in Nicaragua in the forefront of regional consciousness, adding to the national climate that blocked a military invasion of that country.

The Center worked to secure the appointment of a black minister to the public utility company's board of directors, which had been virtually all-white for fifty years. It also coordinated a coalition of citizens' groups that challenged discrimination in lending. Five years of work on this issue resulted in agreements worth over $55 million in new loans for low and moderate income neighborhoods. Key Memphis banks increased their lending in majority black parts of the city three-fold.

The Center organized "toxic tours" to educate the populace about hazardous waste dumps, especially in low income areas of the city. It helped neighborhood organizations negotiate agreements with corporations responsible for proliferating the poisons. It maintained an educational program about the detrimental effects of national military spending on the Memphis area, calling attention to skewered government budget priorities. During the Persian Gulf War it organized a weekly Saturday noon rally for peace in front of the Federal Building in downtown Memphis.

Through the first decade of its existence the Mid-South Peace and Justice Center gained a reputation for being on the cutting edge of political and social justice activities in this part of the country. It did this despite having no golden egg or bountiful benefactor. About half its budget comes from contributions by individuals and organizations in the region. The rest is solicited as grants for particular projects. More than ten years after its optimistic origins, the Mid-South Peace and Justice Center had a staff of four, and a stubborn if sometimes shaky annual budget of a little over $100,000. It was keeping hope alive.

Organizations like MIFA built houses and provided emergency relief. The Peace and Justice Center helped change bank policies so that low-income people could buy houses. It helped change government spending priorities to diminish the need for emergency relief. "We're not jelly makers, we're tree shakers," was the way the Center's Director Hubert Van Tol expressed the difference.

Standing on a river bank watching dead bodies float by, good people will retrieve the bodies and bury them reverently. But it's also important to ask what's happening upstream to cause all the deaths. The bodies need to be buried, but the source of the problem also needs to be addressed. Compassionate people will reach out a helpful, healing hand to the hurting neighbor next door. Compassionate people will also want to know why the neighbor is hurting, and be concerned to alter the source of the hurt. Both approaches are necessary—in Memphis and around the world. And both will be necessary as far into the future as we can see. Good people will take part in either, or both, depending on their time and talents. In whichever direction they move, they can be confident they are enhancing in some modest but real way the well-being of the human family. They are good people doing truly good things. They are spreading *shalom*.

*Our work is to sow. Another generation will be reaping the harvest.*

—Dorothy Day

# CHAPTER TEN

# SOWING NONVIOLENT SEEDS

"Once, in Damascus, when I was strolling along the street called Straight, I watched as a man who was riding slowly through the crowd on a bicycle with a basket of oranges precariously balanced on the handlebars was bumped by a porter so bent by a heavy burden that he had not seen him. The burden was dropped, the oranges scattered and a bitter altercation broke out between the two men, surrounded by a circle of onlookers. After an angry exchange of shouted insults, as the bicyclist moved toward the porter with a clenched fist, a tattered little man slipped from the crowd, took the raised fist in his hands and kissed it. A murmur of approval ran through the watchers, the antagonists relaxed, then the people began picking up the oranges and the little man drifted away."[1]

"In Moscow, in what was then the Soviet Union, hundreds of people gathered outside the Parliament during the August 1991 attempted coup. They built barricades of trolley cars, buses, old pieces of metal and box springs—not so much because that would stop the tanks for more than a few minutes, but to enable them to enter into dialogue with the attacking soldiers. Mothers and girls gave the soldiers cakes, food, kisses and flowers, and asked them not to kill their mothers, sisters, and brothers. One friend brought roses and distributed them to the soldiers and gave them a hug, saying, 'Don't shoot; be kind to the people.'"[2]

THE LITTLE OLD MAN in Damascus might have been a Muslim or Jew or Christian. It didn't matter to the crowd what faith he professed. When he moved into the middle of the disturbance, took the upraised fist in his hands and kissed it, he stopped an ugly altercation. His caring act made a big impression on the agitated onlookers. He had sowed nonviolent seeds on the street called Straight. The women who gave cakes and roses to the soldiers at the Parliament building, the Russian White House, during the attempted coup also sowed nonviolent seeds. The soldiers who took these gifts became emotionally unable to fire on the crowd, and the course of history was changed.

The Johnny Appleseed song begins:

The Lord's been good to me.
And so I thank the Lord
For giving me the things I need,
The sun and the rain and the apple seed.
The Lord's been good to me.

The legend of Johnny Appleseed who wandered through the Midwest in the early years of the 19th century sowing with generous abundance was based on the life of a real person, John

Chapman. As a boy in Massachusetts, he had a habit of wandering away on long trips in search of birds and flowers. In 1801 his wandering took him down the Ohio River, paddling a strange craft of two canoes lashed together and filled with decaying apples. Having brought the apples from the cider presses of western Pennsylvania, John Chapman planted his first apple orchard two miles downriver from Steubenville, Ohio.

After returning to Pennsylvania for more seeds, he continued planting. Besides the apples for which he became famous, John Chapman sowed seeds of many healing herbs and indigenous peoples of the area considered him a great medicine man. Apple orchards flourished in what had been the wilderness of Ohio and Indiana, thanks to the man who became forever known as Johnny Appleseed.

Another seed-sowing image comes from the troublesome terrain of Palestine, half a world away from the fertile fields of Ohio.

> Hear this! A sower went out to sow. And as he sowed, some seed fell on the path, and the birds came and ate it up. Other seed fell on rocky ground, where it had little soil. It sprang up at once, because the soil was not deep. And when the sun rose, it was scorched and it withered for lack of roots. Some seed fell among thorns, and the thorns grew up and choked it, and it produced no grain. And some seed fell on rich soil and produced fruit. It came up and grew and yielded thirty, sixty, and even a hundred-fold (Mark 4:3–8).

When seed-sowing works, as it did in this parable, it's like magic. The seed multiplies thirty, sixty or even a hundred times. The wondrous power packed in tiny seeds interacts with the nutrients in the soil to produce bushels of apples in Indiana, or fields of grain in Galilee.

But before the harvest, the seeds have to be sown. Sometimes that happens by chance, as when the wind blows them. Other times, they're sown scientifically by human beings who know what they're doing. Sowing for a successful harvest takes seeds ripe with potential—and it also takes receptive, fertile soil.

## Nonviolent Seeds

The seeds we're looking at here are seeds of nonviolence. They are alive with the gentle power of Gandhi's *satyagraha*, truth force. They are bursting with the persuasive energy of Martin Luther King's soul force. These seeds are rich with reverence for the global ecosystem that nurtures us all. Kept fertile in our minds and hearts, they consist of an alert awareness of a new way of acting, of a different approach to other human beings and to our planet, different from business as usual. The seeds are not different in the sense of a scientific breakthrough or a newly discovered secret of human behavior. But they are different from the familiar pattern of anxious self-concern, of being swept along by the currents of the moment, of carelessly consuming whatever we want from the soil and air and water around us. These old behaviors are what the prophet Hosea called "sowing the wind and reaping the whirlwind" (8:7).

Instead of self-concern, nonviolent seeds contain compassionate other-concern, such as that shown by the old man in Damascus or the caring women outside the Parliament building in Moscow. Instead of drifting in the currents of the moment, the seeds express a critical awareness of what's going on and a personal perseverance in reaching for truth. They foster what King called a "tough mind," a discerning vision of what needs to be accepted and what needs to be resisted. "The tough mind is sharp and penetrating, breaking through the crust of legends and myths and sifting the true from the false," he wrote.[3] Instead of casual consumption, these seeds generate a prudent and sparing use, trimmed to more spartan needs. Nonviolent seeds nurture a certainty that unchecked exploitation of Earth is poisoning our planet to death. Nonviolent seeds also produce the recognition that returning violence for violence, hatred for hatred, only multiplies trouble. As Gandhi said, "An eye for an eye leaves the whole world blind."

## Fertile Soil

Nonviolent seeds have power to change minds and hearts when the soil on which they're sown is fertile. And it often is, much more often than we might imagine. Gandhi considered nonviolence to be so congruent with human nature that he called it a law of our being. "Nonviolence is the law of our species," he said, "as violence is the law of the brute."[4] He pointed out that the normal pattern of human behavior is nonviolent in the sense that people usually give and take, learn to get along. They routinely make adjustments rather than fight.

> I claim that even now, though the social structure is not based on a conscious acceptance of nonviolence, all the world over people live and retain their possessions on the sufferance of one another. If they had not done so, only the fewest and the most ferocious would have survived. But such is not the case. Families are bound together by ties of love, and so are groups in the so-called civilized society called nations.[5]

Gandhian nonviolence appeals to something deep in our hearts. People really do hunger for decency, even those whose life experiences have made them hard and aggressive.

The sower of nonviolent seed does not let a tough exterior deter from extending a humane hand—and keep extending it, even when met by rebuffs. Gandhi identified this kind of patience as a form of self-suffering. The key element in nonviolent example, he believed, is the willingness to suffer rather than strike back in retaliation. When others became explicitly aware of the power of nonviolence through the example of those who practiced it, they would be receptive and begin incorporating it in their own lives.

> Nobody has probably drawn up more petitions or espoused more forlorn causes than I, and I have come to this fundamental conclusion: that if you want something really important to be done you must not merely satisfy the reason, you must move the heart also. The appeal of reason is more to the head but the penetration of the heart comes from suffering. It opens up the inner understanding. Suffering is the badge of the human race, not the sword.[6]

When our nonviolent seeds fall on the generous and creative side of human nature, they find the fertile soil that, miracle-like, produces the many-fold grain. After sowing them we find—another miracle—that the seeds themselves multiply. Unlike material possessions that diminish by being given away, intangible riches increase when they're shared. If we give away money, we have less of it for ourselves. But when we communicate compassion, when we sidestep an attack and respond with patience, when we live our appreciation of the gifts of nature, we find our nonviolent seeds don't run out—they multiply. We have more of them to give. And those who receive them, when their own ground is fertile, start multiplying them still more.

Just as their increase seems a miracle, the origin of these nonviolent seeds is often a mystery. We don't make them, any more than we make apple seeds. We get them from others, when we're ready for them. Sometimes we have to be well plowed for them to take root in us. And that hurts. But when we're plowed and fertilized and ready, we can receive the seeds gratefully, store them carefully, and sow them generously.

## Seeds from the Sixties

Janice and I were given a few seeds of nonviolence in the late 1960s, shortly before we married. Since 1965 I had been intensely involved in the movement to stop the war in Vietnam. At first I didn't look at it particularly as a nonviolent activity. I just knew on the basis of my study and experience that the war in Vietnam should end. Gradually I began to see the movement not just as anti-war, but as pro-peace. I re-read Pope John XXIII's encyclical *Pacem in Terris*. I began to appreciate the implications of Martin Luther King's nonviolent leadership in the Civil Rights Movement. The peace vision of Pope John and Martin Luther King gave me a new appreciation of what the world could become.

Janice received nonviolent seeds when she was completing her graduate studies at Mundelein College in Chicago. She chose to do her master's thesis on nonviolence, seeing it as an overarching idea for the social concerns we both shared. Her thesis work got me as interested in Gandhi's theories as I was already interested in King's tactics. Gandhi's writings gave a firm foundation to our new peace vision. We came to see the value of nonviolence as a life-affirming and life-changing force. When Janice and I married in 1969, we had no idea if we would have opportunities to sow the nonviolent seeds we had been given. We only realized they were a treasure, to be carefully nurtured.

In the summer of 1970 we moved to Memphis where I had been offered a teaching position and Janice given responsibility to organize an adult education program for Catholics in the city. Shortly after we arrived, the new Diocese of Memphis was created, carving the western third of the state away from the diocese of Nashville. Janice soon met the first bishop, a courtly monsignor from Virginia named Carroll Dozier.

As we got to know him better, we learned he had had a special interest in peace since his years as a theology student in Mussolini-dominated Italy. Now, in Memphis, he wanted to make peace the theme of his first pastoral letter to the people of his new diocese. Janice and I were invited to be part of an advisory group to draft the document. When this group first met with him in the fall of 1971, Bishop Dozier's opening statement to us was that, of course, his pastoral letter would follow Thomas Aquinas, who had specified conditions under which a war could be justified. Months later, when the letter was completed and ready for publication, Bishop Dozier had come to realize, and write, that "war was no longer tolerable for a Christian."[7] In the open dialogue during those working sessions around his dining room table, his thinking had evolved in the direction of nonviolence.

Bishop Dozier's peace pastoral brought him to the attention of a group of Catholics on the East Coast who were planning to start a U.S. section of Pax Christi, the International Catholic Peace Movement. He, along with Bishop Thomas Gumbleton of Detroit, was asked to provide episcopal leadership to this new movement. Bishop Dozier asked Janice and me to accompany him in that early effort. So we became involved in Pax Christi in its first years, and were pleased to join with peace people such as Eileen Egan and Gordon Zahn in helping sow nonviolent seeds throughout the country as the Pax Christi movement spread.

The National Security Seminar at the Army War College gave us plenty of opportunity for quiet nonviolent seed sowing during plenary sessions, small-group discussions, and after-hours socializing. We were surprised when the commanding general, at a reception in his home, greeted us with: "Oh yes, I've heard about you. I want you to know that I, too, am a pacifist. I also believe in peace." Although we disagreed with the general on what it meant to be a pacifist and on the means by which peace was to be achieved, we took satisfaction in his awareness of our contribution during the seminar week.

Several years later we had the opportunity to spend a sabbatical year at Pax Christi's international headquarters in

Antwerp, Belgium, where we met people of peace from around the world. In early 1980 the Pax Christi section in Great Britain arranged for us to travel throughout England while I gave a series of lectures on nonviolence. In Leeds, after I spoke about the influence of Gandhi in the liberation of India, a proper gentleman in the back of the room stood up. "Sir, what you are saying is new to me. I have always been under the impression that we British, led by our liberal Prime Minister Clement Atlee, granted India its independence on our own." He was surprised to hear that Gandhian nonviolence had anything to do with it.

Later that year I was a member of the Pax Christi delegation that traveled to the Soviet Union for a theological dialogue with representatives of the Russian Orthodox church. The subject was Christianity and peace. Many times during those talks at the Moscow Theological Seminary in Zagorsk the Pax Christi representatives were able to bring in the nonviolent implications of the gospel.

In 1981 Janice and I participated in a Study Mission to Israel with the organization of American Professors for Peace in the Middle East. For two weeks throughout that country we dialogued with intense Israelis and passionate Palestinians as well as concerned colleagues with whom we traveled. Although we felt that troubled land was a most difficult environment for nonviolent solutions, we did find a few courageous men and women committed to pursuing its path. Most of our personal seeds seemed to have fallen on rocky ground, over there. Then, several years later, the Intifada, the largely nonviolent Palestinian noncooperation movement, began. We have followed it with interest.

In Memphis we joined with other peace people in starting the Mid-South Peace and Justice Center. The first time the nuclear White Train came through Memphis we helped organize a grim greeting as the train entered the city after crossing the Mississippi River. Several of our friends stood on the tracks and succeeded in stopping the train for a few minutes. The local and national news media picked up our nonviolent message. We had other chances to sow nonviolent seeds in our dialogues with officials of the Burlington-Northern railroad that supplied the engines and tracks for the nuclear train.

Through the Peace and Justice Center we came in contact with Howard and Alice Frazier of Promoting Enduring Peace, the Woodmont, Connecticut-based organization, which for years had sponsored International Peace Cruises in the Soviet Union. In 1988 they organized a similar cruise with Soviet and American passengers down the lower Mississippi River from St. Louis to New Orleans. Janice was invited to take part. The following year she was a guest on the Peace Cruise on the Dnieper River in Ukraine, and in 1990 both of us were asked to join that cruise as resource people. We have been able to sow some nonviolent seeds—usually involving considerable learning on our part—in homes in Ukraine and Russia, and through arranging visits to Memphis of people we met there. Our seed sowing and seed receiving continued in our international correspondence with people we have been privileged to meet in Europe, Asia, and Latin America, including an Ethiopian student in Kiev, and an elderly Chinese man from Beijing.

It was on the Mississippi cruise that Janice learned of the arrival in this country of Arun Gandhi, grandson of the Mahatma. He and his wife Sunanda, after their own children were grown and married, came here to complete research on a book. His intention was to compare apartheid in South Africa, India's treatment of the Untouchables, and American racism. Arun and his wife knew the first two from their own life experiences. They had quietly taken up residence at the University of Mississippi to study the third. Arun Gandhi had harbored a desire to begin an institute devoted to studying and teaching the ideals of nonviolence in the spirit of his grandfather, and wanted it located at a university. Janice and I were able to facilitate this move. In June 1991, Arun and Sunanda came to Memphis to begin the M.K. Gandhi Institute for Nonviolence, hosted by Christian Brothers University where I teach.

# Seeds for All

We can sow nonviolent seeds in our microcosm, the everyday world in which we live and move and have our being. Every one of our personal interactions can be engaged in with a greater degree of sensitivity, with a conscious effort to avoid words or deeds that hurt, and an equally conscious effort to say and do what will help. "In the end, it is the reality of personal relationships that saves everything," Thomas Merton wrote. One of Janice's and my favorite stories is the Buddhist Parable of the Tiger:

> There was once a man who was crossing a field and met a tiger. He ran to a great cliff and caught hold of a root and swung over the side of the cliff. But at the bottom of the cliff was another tiger. Soon two little mice came along and began to gnaw on the vine. The man looked in terror at the tiger below. But then he saw a strawberry vine. He picked a strawberry and ate it. How delicious it was![8]

We often remind each other, in times of stress, to pick a strawberry; it tastes so good. Once in a while we share the Tiger story with others. It never fails to provoke a smile and reduce some of the tension that so often builds up in these pressing times.

We can also sow nonviolent seeds in the macrocosm, the wide world that is our full human habitat. We can engage in community building, in modeling nonviolent conflict resolution, in making others aware of the suffering of migrant laborers. We can stop the nuclear trucks as we earlier stopped the nuclear train. And there might come a time of rare opportunity to exert significant change: ending a famine, averting a genocide, converting to clean energy. The possibilities are limitless. The fields are vast. The seeds are potent. And the results can be awe-inspiring. This is the way a great teacher put it: "A man scatters seed on the ground. Night and day, whether he sleeps or gets up, the seed sprouts and grows, though he does not know how. All by itself the soil produces grain—first the stalk, then the head, then the full kernel in the head" (Mark 4:26–28).

"This," Jesus said, "is what the Kingdom of God is like."

# Conclusion

A VISION OF PEACE for the dawn of the 21st century has two aspects: the world as it is, and the world as it can become. As it is, the world is troubled. People are suffering. We in the United States no longer have the Communist Enemy to distract us. The Cold War is over. We have lost the luxury of business as usual with the excuse of an omnipresent Enemy against whom our national resources had to be directed. We can now face the world as it really is. And we can't blame that Enemy for the world not being right the way it is. To acknowledge that the world is not right is the beginning of inner peace. A person cannot experience genuine personal peace without first seeing with wide-open eyes the suffering that is part of the fabric of human existence. Much of it is of human agency. Much of it happens through the involvement, usually involuntary, of "good" people. Much of it happens also because "good" people do nothing, or not enough, to change things for the better.

We have seen something of the dark forces lurking in the

Shadow of our psyche that blind us to the implications of our actions. We've looked, too, at the tangled web of sexuality that all too often has repressing and harassing results. And we've also seen something of the powerful imperatives operating in our milieu to push good people into accommodation with harsh and harmful forces. Imperatives from technology create isolating, individualizing telecommunications and weapons of mass destruction. Imperatives from economics exert relentless forces for improving income, regardless of who is put out of business or who suffers when the business is moved to a low-cost area of the world.

The power imperative drives people—and nations—to seek ever more persuasive and more unshakable ways of bending others' lives to our will. Developing a coherent philosophy of life carries the danger of becoming a rigid ideology which would impose behavior patterns on others, going so far as to punish or kill them if they refuse to conform. And even reaching out a helping hand to those who are hurting can become a charity imperative impeding other efforts to eliminate the causes of hurt.

The other aspect of the peace vision is what we do to make things better. The prerequisite for anything along these lines has to be a desire for good faith, a genuine effort to see the world as clearly as possible. Then, as we realize we've been gifted with an energy called compassion, we start to make a difference when we see the opportunities every day to reach out and help someone. We start to make a difference when we put into practice the alternatives to violence in our speech, our family life, our professional interactions that are readily available. And we definitely make a difference when we join our efforts with other like-minded people and experience the healing power that comes from a reinforcing community spirit. A multitude of good people in many countries is already working to make things better.

There is no magic answer, no golden key about what to do to make this world a substantially better place. Utopian visions have come and gone. Maybe the twenty-first century will bring the definitive solution, but I'm not counting on it. What we do have, though, are inspiring dreams:

—Martin Luther King's dream that one day people will be judged not by the color of their skin but by the content of their character.

—Gandhi's dream of friendship with the whole world.

—Dom Helder Camara's dream of a millennium without misery.

—Dorothy Day's dream of sowing nonviolent seeds for the harvest others will reap.

One thing is certain. Each one of us has something to contribute to the realization of these dreams. We may not change the world, but we don't have to leave it the same, either.

# NOTES

## CHAPTER ONE: WHO WE GOOD PEOPLE ARE

1. Ralph McGehee, *Deadly Deceits: My 25 Years in the CIA* (New York: Sheridan Square Publications, 1983), p. 13.

2. Rick Fields, *The Code of the Warrior: In History, Myth, and Everyday Life* (New York: HarperCollins, Harper Perennial, 1991), p. 264.

3. "Jail sentence brings apology," *The Commercial Appeal*, Memphis, Aug. 16, 1992, p. B-2.

4. President Bill Clinton used those words, "good people," to characterize veterans of the Vietnam War just before his 1993 Memorial Day speech at the Vietnam War Memorial in Washington: "I do believe that our policy was wrong, but that doesn't mean that the people who were committed to the United States and to doing what they were ordered to do by the commander-in-chief weren't good people. They were good people." "Clinton says he 'can't run away from' Vietnam letter," *The Commercial Appeal*, Memphis, May 31, 1993, p. A-2.

5. This story is told in Janne E. Nolan, *Guardians of the Arsenal: The Politics of Nuclear Strategy* (New York: HarperCollins, A New Republic Book, 1989), p. 129.

6. Robert Jay Lifton and Eric Markusan, *The Genocidal Mentality: Nazi Holocaust and Nuclear Threat* (New York: Basic Books, 1990), p. 134.

7. For a detailed, although generally sympathetic, account of CIA activities that include violating moral norms, the book *Inside the CIA: Revealing the Secrets of the World's Most Powerful Spy Agency*, by Ronald Kessler, is helpful (New York: Simon and Schuster, Pocket Books, 1992).

8. *General Electric Company Annual Report 1983*, p. 27.

9. *Ibid.*, p. 5.

## CHAPTER TWO: THOSE WE HURT

1. From Donald L. Barlett and James B. Steele, *America: What Went Wrong?* (Kansas City: Andrews and McMeel, 1992), p. 3.

2. From Gerard and Janice Vanderhaar, *The Philippines: Agony and Hope* (Erie, Penn.: Pax Christi USA, 1989), p. 17.

3. Mohandas K. Gandhi, *An Autobiography: The Story of My Experiments with Truth* (Boston: Beacon Press, 1957, 13th printing, 1972), p. 349.

4. "Sentenced," *The Commercial Appeal*, Memphis, Sept. 15, 1992, p. A-2.

5. Details about the Akosombo dam and its financing are given in *Conditions of Peace: An Inquiry*, edited by Michael Shuman and Julia Sweig (Washington, D.C.: EXPRO Press, 1991), pp. 183-84.

6. These statistics are given in Ruth Leger Sivard, *World Military and Social Expenditures 1991* (Washington, D.C.: World Priorities, 1991), p. 59.

7. William Greider, *Who Will Tell the People?: The Betrayal of American Democracy* (New York: Simon and Schuster, 1992), p. 380.

8. This incident was reported in Steve Brouwer, *Conquest and Capitalism 1492-1992* (Carlisle, Penn.: Big Picture Books, 1992), p. 80.

9. The summary of U.S. business interests in Guatemala is taken from *Dollars and Dictators: A Guide to Central America*, by Tom Barry, Beth Wood, and Deb Preusch (Albuquerque, N.M.: The Resource Center, 1982), p. 125.

10. This incident was reported on p. 2 of the October 18, 1991 *Central America Newsline* of Witness for Peace (2201 P St., NW, Washington, D.C. 20037).

11. This incident was reported on p. 3 of the January 22, 1992 *Central America Newsline* of Witness for Peace.

12. *Land Conflicts in Brazil* (Antwerp, Belgium: Pax Christi International, 1988), p. 16.

13. Janice McLaughlin, M.M., "Famine Strikes Again," *Maryknoll*, Sept. 1992, pp. 26-31.

14. Quoted in Al Levin, "Beneath the Burden of World Debt," *The Catholic Worker*, June-July 1989, p. 1.

15. This story is told on p. 3 of the May 1992 issue of *Blueprint for Social Justice*, published by the Twomney Center of Loyola University, New Orleans.

## CHAPTER THREE: WHY WE DO THESE THINGS

1. "More than 1000 will lose jobs, says NW," *The Commercial Appeal*, Memphis, Jan. 5, 1993, p. A-1.

2. Frank Harvey, *Air War—Vietnam* (New York: Bantam Books, 1967), p. 115.

3. *America: What Went Wrong?*, pp. 34-35.

4. *Who Will Tell the People?*, p. 394.

5. Column "Ashe's story wasn't easy to tell, but it needed to be told," by Al Dunning, *The Commercial Appeal*, Memphis, April 15, 1992, p. D-1.

6. Richard J. Barnet, *The Rockets' Red Glare: War, Politics and the American*

*Presidency* (New York: Simon and Schuster, 1990), p. 376.

7. Details about delayed deaths of Iraqi children are given by Elizabeth Ryden Benjamin, "Watching Children Die," *Fellowship*, July/Aug. 1991, pp. 22 ff.

8. "Pentagon stresses U.S. role: Policy sees superpower dominating the world," *The Sun-Sentinal*, Ft. Lauderdale, Mar. 8, 1992, p. 3-A.

9. *The Rockets' Red Glare*, p. 380.

10. Walter Wink, *Engaging the Powers: Discernment and Resistance in a World of Domination* (Minneapolis: Fortress Press, 1992), p. 42.

11. Quoted in Matthew Fox, *A Spirituality Named Compassion* (San Francisco: Harper & Row, 1990), pp. 69-70.

12. Column "Putting on a happy face" by George Will, *The Commercial Appeal*, Memphis, July 14, 1992, p. A-8.

13. Martin Luther King, Jr., *Strength to Love* (Philadelphia: Fortress Press, 1981), p. 34.

## CHAPTER FOUR: THE SHADOW KNOWS

1. Bill Buford. *Among the Thugs: The Experience, and the Seduction, of Crowd Violence* (New York and London: W.W. Norton, 1991), p. 187.

2. Helen Caldicott, *Missile Envy: The Arms Race and Nuclear War* (New York: Bantam Books, 1986 edition), p. 262.

3. William Barrett, *Irrational Man: A Study in Existential Philosophy* (Garden City, N.Y.: Doubleday Anchor Book, 1958), p. 276.

4. Quoted in Israel Charny, *How Can We Commit the Unthinkable? Genocide: The Human Cancer* (Boulder, Colo.: Westview Press, 1982), p. 72.

5. "Peasant Woman Stomped to Death by GI's at My Lai, Sergeant Writes," by Seymour M. Hersh, *Philadelphia Bulletin*, Dec. 2, 1969, in Charny, *op. cit.*, pp. 182-83.

6. This incident was reported in the *Jerusalem Press Daily Report*, April 22, 1992, reprinted in "Breaking the Siege: The Newsletter of the Middle East Justice Network," P.O. Box 558, Cambridge, MA 02238, June-July 1992, p. 12.

7. Sam Keen, *Faces of the Enemy: Reflections of the Hostile Imagination* (San Francisco: Harper & Row, 1986), p. 11.

8. "Communities acquire look of fortresses," *The Commercial Appeal*, Memphis, July 28, 1992, p. A-9.

9. Charny, *op. cit.*, p. 105.

10. Christopher R. Browning, *Ordinary Men: Reserve Police Battalion 101 and the Final Solution in Poland* (New York: HarperCollins, 1992), p. 64.

11. *Ibid.*

12. Charny, *op. cit.*, p. 74.

## CHAPTER FIVE: THE S-WORD

1. "Pentagon rips officers for Tailhook debauchery," *The Commercial Appeal*,

Memphis, April 24, 1993, p. A-1.

2. Laura Coleman, a reporter for the Memphis *Commercial Appeal*, helped stop a man from jumping off a bridge in Memphis. Her account of what happened, "'Tired' man talked out of bridge jump" appeared in *The Commercial Appeal* on Jan. 31, 1993, p. A-1.

3. Paul B. Brown, *In and For the World: Bringing the Contemporary Into Christian Worship* (Minneapolis: Fortress Press, 1992), pp. 120-21.

4. Charny, *op. cit.*, pp. 114-15.

5. "Military is afraid to admit 'sissies' can be brave, too," by Richard Rodriguez, *National Catholic Reporter*, Feb. 12, 1993, p. 15.

6. Bruce Kokopeli and George Lakey, "More Power Than We Want: Masculine Sexuality and Violence." This article first appeared in *Win* magazine in July, 1976. It was reprinted as the only contribution by men in *Reweaving the Web of Life: Feminism and Nonviolence*, edited by Pam McAllister (Philadelphia: New Society Publishers, 1982). The quote is found on pp. 236-37 of this book.

7. Caldicott, *Missile Envy*, p. 263.

8. Cynthia Adcock, "Fear of 'Other': The Common Root of Sexism and Militarism," in *Reweaving the Web of Life*, p. 217.

9. Quoted in Cynthia Enloe, *Does Khaki Become You? The Militarization of Women's Lives* (Boston: South End Press, 1983), pp. 153-54.

10. Cynthia Enloe, "A Feminist Perspective on Foreign Military Bases," in *The Sun Never Sets: Confronting the Network of Foreign U.S. Military Bases*, edited by Joseph Gerson and Bruce Birchard (Boston: South End Press, 1991), p. 101.

11. William Broyles, Jr., "Sex and the workplace," in the *Miami Herald*, Oct. 20, 1991, p. 6-C.

12. *Summa Theologica*, Part I, Question 92, response to Objection 1.

## CHAPTER SIX: PERSONAL SALVATION

1. From "Waste-oil tycoon fights bills for toxic cleanup," *The Commercial Appeal*, Memphis, July 19, 1992, p. A-1.

2. From "Grace Mojtabai found business brisk and the Lord nigh in Amarillo as Pantex prepared for doomsday," *National Catholic Reporter*, Aug. 1, 1986, pp. 9-12.

3. Gerard Thomas Straub, *Salvation for Sale: An Insider's View of Pat Robertson's Ministry* (Buffalo: Prometheus Books, 1986), p. 9.

4. Sidney E. Ahlstrom, *A Religious History of the American People* (Garden City, N.Y., Doubleday Image Books, 1975), vol. 2, p. 251.

5. Dogmatic Constitution on the Church *(Lumen Gentium)*, section 9, from *The Documents of Vatican II*, edited by Walter M. Abbott, S.J. (New York: Guild Press, America Press, Association Press, 1966), p. 25.

6. Passion Sunday sermon at the National Cathedral (Episcopal) in Washington, D.C. on Mar. 31, 1968, contained in *A Testament of Hope: The*

*Essential Writings and Speeches of Martin Luther King, Jr.*, edited by James M. Washington (New York: HarperCollins paperback edition, 1991), p. 269.

7. Paper "In Search of the Salvific Value of a Political Praxis of Peace" delivered by Edward Schillebeeckx, O.P., at the Pax Christi International Congress on Peace Spirituality, in Nassogne, Belgium, Oct. 9-11, 1981. Published in *Peace Spirituality for Peacemakers* (Antwerp, Belgium: Omega Press, 1985), p. 25.

8. *Who Will Tell the People?*, p. 307.

9. Joyce Nelson, *The Perfect Machine: Television and the Bomb* (Philadelphia: New Society Publishers, 1992), p. 168.

10. Quoted in *The Rebirth of America*, edited by Nancy Leigh DeMoss (Philadelphia: Arthur S. DeMoss Foundation, 1986), p. 78.

11. A comprehensive assessment of the Religious Right's agenda is given in Samuel S. Hill and Dennis E. Owen, *The New Religious/Political Right in America* (Nashville: Abingdon, 1982).

12. Quoted in the "Grace Mojtabai...Pantex" article, p. 11.

13. Pastoral Constitution on the Church in the Modern World (*Gaudium et Spes*), section 26, in *The Documents of Vatican II*, p. 225.

## CHAPTER SEVEN: BAD FAITH AND GOOD FAITH

1. "Iraq seeks bodies of buried troops," *The Commercial Appeal*, Memphis, Sept. 16, 1991, p. A-2.

2. *The Genocidal Mentality*, p. 131.

3. The classic source for Sartre's analysis of bad faith and good faith is his book *Being and Nothingness*. My summary is based on an article by Joseph Catalano, "Authenticity: A Sartrean Perspective," in *The Philosophical Forum*, Vol. XXII, No. 2, Winter, 1990, pp. 99-119.

4. *The Genocidal Mentality*, p. 13.

5. Charny, *op. cit.*, p. 26.

6. David Ray Griffin, "Postmodern Theology as First-World Liberation Theology," the 1991 Paine Lecture in Religion at the University of Missouri-Columbia, published by the University of Missouri.

## CHAPTER EIGHT: THE GIFT OF COMPASSION

1. From Jean-Bertrand Aristide, *In the Parish of the Poor: Writings from Haiti* (Maryknoll, N.Y.: Orbis Books, 1990), pp. 3-4.

2. From the Introduction by J.G. Gaarlandt to *An Interrupted Life: The Diaries of Etty Hillesum 1941-43* (New York: Simon and Schuster, Pocket Books edition, 1985), p. xv.

3. Quoted in Robert McAfee Brown, "The Holocaust as a Problem in Moral Choice," *A Peace Reader: Essential Readings on War, Justice, Non-violence and World Order*, edited by Joseph J. Fahey and Richard Armstrong (Mahwah, N.J.: Paulist Press, revised edition, 1992), p. 238.

4. Samuel P. Oliner and Pearl M. Oliner, *The Altruistic Personality: Rescuers of Jews in Nazi Europe* (New York: Macmillan, The Free Press, 1988), p. 164.

5. *Ibid.*, p. 165.

6. *The Genocidal Mentality*, p. 272.

7. Eileen Egan, *Such a Vision of the Street: Mother Teresa—The Spirit and the Work* (Garden City, N.Y.: Doubleday, 1985), p. 24.

8. From the Journals of Thomas Merton, quoted in Michael Mott, *The Seven Mountains of Thomas Merton* (Boston: Houghton Mifflin, 1984), p. 111.

9. From *The Wisdom of China and India*, edited by Lin Yutang (New York: Random House, Modern Library, 1942), pp. 367-68.

10. *The Genocidal Mentality*, p. 259.

## CHAPTER NINE: GOOD PEOPLE DOING GOOD THINGS

1. From "Ex-gang members learn Brown's positive thinking," *The Commercial Appeal*, Memphis, Oct. 6, 1991, p. A-6.

2. From Michael True, *To Construct Peace: 30 More Justice Seekers, Peace Makers* (Mystic, Conn., Twenty-Third Publications, 1992), pp. 72-73.

3. Details of Clara Hale's contributions are contained in her obituary in *The New York Times*: "Clara Hale, 97, Who Aided Addicts' Babies, Dies" (Dec. 20, 1992), p. Y-17.

4. Quoted in *The Power of the People*, edited by Robert Cooney and Helen Michalowski (Culver City, Cal.: Peace Press, 1977), p. 171.

5. Quoted in Michael True, *Justice Seekers, Peace Makers: 32 Portraits in Courage* (Mystic, Conn.: Twenty-Third Publications, 1985), pp. 32-33.

6. Dr. King's last sermon, on the eve of his assassination, delivered at Mason Temple in Memphis, Tennessee on April 3, 1968, contained in *A Testament of Hope*, pp. 279-86. This quote is on p. 285.

## CHAPTER TEN: SOWING NONVIOLENT SEEDS

1. From a letter to *The New York Times* by Kenneth W. Morgan, Jan. 30, 1991.

2. From David Hartsough, "Faces of Courage and Hope," in *Ground Zero*, the newspaper of the Ground Zero community in Bangor, Washington, Winter, 1992, pp. 7-8.

3. *Strength to Love*, p. 2.

4. Gandhi expressed this thought many times. The quote here is from *Nonviolent Resistance*, by M.K. Gandhi (New York: Schocken Books, 1961), p. 133.

5. *All Men Are Brothers: Life and Thoughts of Mahatma Gandhi as Told in His Own Words*, edited by Krishna Kripalani (Ahmedabad, India: Navajivan Publishing House, 1950), p. 113.

6. *Ibid.*, p. 118.

7. "Peace: Gift and Task," Pastoral Letter to the people of the Diocese of Memphis, by Most Reverend Carroll T. Dozier, D.D., Bishop of Memphis, pub-

lished by the Diocese of Memphis, Dec., 1971. This quote is on p. 11.

8. This story is contained in Leonard J. Biallas, *Myths: Gods, Heroes, and Saviors* (Mystic, Conn.: Twenty-Third Publications, 1986), pp. 250-51.

# BIBLIOGRAPHY

Arendt, Hannah. *Eichmann in Jerusalem: A Report on the Banality of Evil.* New York: Viking Press, 1963.

Aristide, Jean-Bertrand. *In the Parish of the Poor: Writings from Haiti.* Maryknoll, N.Y.: Orbis Books, 1990.

Barlett, Donald L., and James B. Steele, *America: What Went Wrong?* Kansas City: Andrews and McMeel, 1992.

Barnet, Richard J. *The Rockets' Red Glare: War, Politics and the American Presidency.* New York: Simon and Schuster, 1990.

Barry, Tom, Beth Wood, and Deb Preusch. *Dollars and Dictators: A Guide to Central America.* Albuquerque, N.M.: The Resource Center, 1982.

Bernards, Neal, and Terry O'Neill, eds. *Male/Female Roles: Opposing Viewpoints.* San Diego: Greenhaven Press, 1989.

Bly, Robert. *Iron John: A Book About Men.* Reading, Mass.: Addison-Wesley, 1990.

Brouwer, Steve. *Conquest and Capitalism 1492-1992.* Carlisle, Penn.: Big Picture Books, 1992.

Brown, Paul B. *In and For the World: Bringing the Contemporary Into Christian Worship.* Minneapolis: Fortress Press, 1992.

Browning, Christopher R. *Ordinary Men: Reserve Police Battalion 101 and the Final Solution in Poland.* New York: HarperCollins, 1992.

Buford, Bill. *Among the Thugs: The Experience, and the Seduction, of Crowd Violence.* New York and London: W.W. Norton, 1991.

Caldicott, Helen. *Missile Envy: The Arms Race and Nuclear War.* New York: Bantam Books, 1986.

Carmody, John. *What Women Don't Understand About Men and Vice Versa.* Mystic, Conn.: Twenty-Third Publications, 1992.

Charny, Israel. *How Can We Commit the Unthinkable? Genocide: The Human Cancer.* Boulder, Colo.: Westview Press, 1982.

Cooney, Robert, and Helen Michalowski. *The Power of the People.* Culver City, Cal.: Peace Press, 1977.

Dellinger, David. *Vietnam Revisited: Covert Action to Invasion to Reconstruction.* Boston: South End Press, 1986.

DeMoss, Nancy Leigh, ed. *The Rebirth of America*. Philadelphia: Arthur S. DeMoss Foundation, 1986.

Dowd, Michael. *Earthspirit: A Handbook for Nurturing an Ecological Christianity*. Mystic, Conn.: Twenty-Third Publications, 1991.

Egan, Eileen. *Such a Vision of the Street: Mother Teresa—The Spirit and the Work*. Garden City, N.Y.: Doubleday, 1985.

Enloe, Cynthia. *Does Khaki Become You? The Militarization of Women's Lives*. Boston: South End Press, 1983.

Fahey, Joseph J., and Richard Armstrong, eds. *A Peace Reader: Essential Readings on War, Justice, Non-violence and World Order*. Mahwah, N.J.: Paulist Press, revised edition, 1992.

Fields, Rick. *The Code of the Warrior: In History, Myth, and Everyday Life*. New York: HarperCollins, Harper Perennial, 1991.

Fox, Matthew. *A Spirituality Named Compassion*. San Francisco: Harper & Row, 1990.

Fox, Thomas C. *Iraq: Military Vistory, Moral Defeat*. Kansas City: Sheed and Ward, 1991.

Gandhi, Mohandas K. *An Autobiography: The Story of My Experiments with Truth*. Boston: Beacon Press, 1957.

Gandhi, M.K. *Non-violent Resistance*. New York: Schocken Books, 1961.

Gerson, Joseph, and Bruce Birchard. *The Sun Never Sets: Confronting the Network of Foreign U.S. Military Bases*. Boston: South End Press, 1991.

Greider, William. *Who Will Tell the People?: The Betrayal of American Democracy*. New York: Simon and Schuster, 1992.

Haas, Peter J. *Morality After Auschwitz: The Radical Challenge of the Nazi Ethic*. Philadelphia: Fortress Press, 1988.

Harvey, Frank. *Air War—Vietnam*. New York: Bantam Books, 1967.

Hill, Samuel S., and Dennis E. Owen.*The New Religious/Political Right in America*. Nashville: Abingdon, 1982.

Keen, Sam. *Faces of the Enemy: Reflections of the Hostile Imagination*. San Francisco: Harper & Row, 1986.

Kessler, Ronald. *Inside the CIA: Revealing the Secrets of the World's Most Powerful Spy Agency*. New York: Simon and Schuster, Pocket Books, 1992.

King, Martin Luther, Jr. *Strength to Love*. Philadelphia: Fortress Press, 1981.

Kripalani, Krishna, ed. *All Men Are Brothers: Life and Thoughts of Mahatma Gandhi as Told in His Own Words*. Ahmedabad, India: Navajivan Publishing House, 1950.

Lifton, Robert Jay, and Eric Markusan. *The Genocidal Mentality: Nazi Holocaust and Nuclear Threat*. New York: Basic Books, 1990.

McAllister, Pam, ed. *Reweaving the Web of Life: Feminism and Nonviolence*. Philadelphia: New Society Publishers, 1982.

McGehee, Ralph. *Deadly Deceits: My 25 Years in the CIA*. New York: Sheridan Square Publications, 1983.

McManus, Philip, and Gerald Schlabach, eds. *Relentless Persistence: Nonviolent Actions in Latin America*. Philadelphia: New Society Publishers, 1991.

McSorley, Richard, S.J. *It's a Sin to Build a Nuclear Weapon: The Collected Works on War and Christian Peacemaking*. Baltimore: Fortkamp, 1991.

Mott, Michael. *The Seven Mountains of Thomas Merton*. Boston: Houghton Mifflin, 1984.

Nelson, Joyce. *The Perfect Machine: Television and the Bomb*. Philadelphia: New Society Publishers, 1992.

Nelson-Pallmeyer, Jack. *Brave New World Order: Must We Pledge Allegiance?* Maryknoll, N.Y.: Orbis Books, 1992.

Nolan, Janne E. *Guardians of the Arsenal: The Politics of Nuclear Strategy*. New York: HarperCollins, A New Republic Book, 1989.

O'Gorman, Angie, ed. *The Universe Bends Toward Justice: A Reader on Christian Nonviolence in the U.S.* Philadelphia: New Society Publishers, 1990.

Oliner, Samuel P. and Pearl M. Oliner. *The Altruistic Personality: Rescuers of Jews in Nazi Europe*. New York: The Free Press (Macmillan), 1988.

Reardon, Betty A. *Sexism and the War System*. New York: Columbia University Teachers College Press, 1985.

Shuman, Michael and Julia Sweig, eds. *Conditions of Peace: An Inquiry*. Washington, D.C.: EXPRO Press, 1991.

Straub, Gerard Thomas. *Salvation for Sale: An Insider's View of Pat Robertson's Ministry*. Buffalo: Prometheus Books, 1986.

True, Michael. *Justice Seekers, Peace Makers: 32 Portraits in Courage*. Mystic, Conn.: Twenty-Third Publications, 1985.

True, Michael. *To Construct Peace: 30 More Justice Seekers, Peace Makers*. Mystic, Conn.: Twenty-Third Publications, 1992.

Vanderhaar, Gerard. *Active Nonviolence: A Way of Personal Peace*. Mystic, Conn.: Twenty-Third Publications, 1990.

Vanderhaar, Gerard and Janice. *The Philippines: Agony and Hope*. Erie, Penn.: Pax Christi-USA, 1989.

Washington, James M. *A Testament of Hope: The Essential Writings and Speeches of Martin Luther King, Jr.* New York: HarperCollins, paperback edition, 1991.

Wink, Walter. *Engaging the Powers: Discernment and Resistance in a World of Domination*. Minneapolis: Fortress Press, 1992.

# Of Related Interest...

## Morality and Its Beyond
Dick Westley
Fresh insights into the meaning of morality. Encourages a "pastoral morality" within the church.

ISBN: 0-89622-207-1, 324 pp, $8.95

## Catholic Morality Revisited
*Origins and Contemporary Challenges*
Gerard S. Sloyan
Valuable resource for those who are confused about the meaning of morality and for those who teach and counsel them.

ISBN: 0-89622-418-x, 160 pp, $9.95

## The Harm We Do
*A Catholic Doctor Confronts Church, Moral, and Medical Teaching*
Joyce Poole
Looks at the conflicts that arise between church teaching and capabilities based on technological advances.

ISBN: 0-89622-543-7, 168 pp, $12.95

## To Construct Peace
*30 More Justice Seekers, Peace Makers*
Michael True
Unique insights into the lives of those devoted to nonviolent social change.

ISBN: 0-89622-487-2, 208 pp, $9.95

## Proclaiming Justice & Peace
*Papal Documents from Rerum Novarum to Centesimus Annus*
edited by Michael Walsh and Brian Davies
The tradition of the church's social teaching over the past 100 years—14 documents in all—are presented and explained.

ISBN: 0-89622-548-8, 512 pp, $19.95